AFRICAN GENESIS

Folk Tales and Myths of Africa

AFRICAN GENESIS
Folk Tales and Myths of Africa

LEO FROBENIUS

AND

DOUGLAS C. FOX

DOVER PUBLICATIONS, INC.
Mineola, New York

Published in Canada by General Publishing Company, Ltd., 30 Lesmill Road, Don Mills, Toronto, Ontario.

Bibliographical Note

This Dover edition, first published in 1999, is an unabridged and unaltered republication of the work originally published by Stackpole Sons, New York, in 1937 under the title *African Genesis*.

Library of Congress Cataloging-in-Publication Data

Frobenius, Leo, 1873–1938.
  African genesis : folk tales and myths of Africa / Leo Frobenius and Douglas C. Fox.
    p.   cm.
  ISBN 0-486-40911-2 (pbk.)
  1. Tales—Africa. 2. Mythology, African. I. Fox, Douglas C. (Douglas Claughton), 1906–   . II. Title.
GR350.F745   1999
398.2'096—dc21   99-32762
                                                                            CIP

Manufactured in the United States of America
Dover Publications, Inc., 31 East 2nd Street, Mineola, N.Y. 11501

CONTENTS

PART TWO: THE SUDANESE

PART THREE : SOUTHERN RHODESIANS

NOTE ON THE ILLUSTRATIONS

The illustrations in this book are taken from material in the archives of the *Forschungsinstitut für Kulturmorphologie in Frankfurt am Main*. They are the work of Fräulein Kate Marr, one of the institute's staff artists.

The full page portraits of natives were drawn on various African expeditions of the Frobenius staff during which their stories were set down.

AFRICAN GENESIS

Folk Tales and Myths of Africa

FOREWORD

THE facsimiles of rock paintings and the portraits reproduced in this book are part of a remarkable series of collections in Frankfort-on-Main, assembled under the direction of Professor Leo Frobenius — the Prehistoric Rock Picture Gallery.

Together with the anthropological writings of Professor Frobenius, this collection offers the most persuasive evidence of a common prehistoric culture of African and European races. Some forty years ago a French scholar, Riviere, made a discovery embarrassing to the important anthropologists of Europe. He found pictures in a cave of Northern Spain that had been painted in the Ice Age, and the quality of the art showed that Ice Age man had attained a culture and a level in art not so very far from our own. It was irritating to modern European scientists to think that any "primitive" culture could compare with the grandeur and ultimate splendor of nineteenth century Europe's. What is more, it had generally been thought that the older Stone Age culture, which showed little relationship to cultures of the post-glacial period, had disappeared when the ice receded northward. Young Leo Frobenius, a student who had no inhibited regard for his own cultural world as the best of all possible worlds, asked himself, in the light of the discovery of the cave picture, whether it might not have been possible for this older Stone Age culture to have been indigenous to Africa as well as to Europe. It did not seem likely to young Frobenius that anything so alive as that culture could disappear. He recalled the fact that North Africa had not always been a desert, and that it might well have nourished a human culture at a time when glaciers still covered the southern Pyrenees. Moreover, it was thought that Spain had been part of Africa and Europe at that time, with no Straits of Gibraltar between the continents.

The South Africans still paint rock pictures, so ran Frobenius' thought. Was it possible that the culture of old could still be alive today, declined, of course, but still a remainder of a culture which had once flourished in Spain?

The organization and the anthropological pioneering which produced the evidence to confirm the original Frobenius hypothesis is familiar history to scientists. It has become part of popular knowledge since the exhibit of Frobenius' work in such institutions as the Museum of Modern Art in New York, and Professor Frobenius' name seems destined to outshine the most brilliant luminaries of modern anthropology. Back of that career, however, lies a philosophical breadth and a singleness of purpose most extraordinary in scholars whose work is so specialized.

Frobenius once said, "We modern Europeans, concentrating on the newspaper and on that which happens from one day to the next, have lost the ability to think in large dimensions. We need a change in *Lebensgefuhl* (our feeling for life). It is my hope that the enormous perspective of human growth which has been opened to us by these rock pictures and by the research of the modern prehistorian may serve to contribute in some small measure to its development."

When the rock picture research of Frobenius' expeditions led him to symbols and drawings which indicated a transfusion of cultures and faiths between African and Egyptian civilizations and among other races, it became necessary for him to understand the mythology back of the paintings. In many cases in Africa this necessitated taking down the native folk tales and myths and relating the stories and superstitions back to the paintings. This body of folklore, authentic and imaginative, is the substance of the present volume.

Nothing offers a better insight into the character of Frobenius than his proposals written to Adolf Bastian, one of the great German scholars, at the time of the discovery by Riviere.*

1. The most difficult obstacle to our understanding of culture is our ignorance. We do not know enough. Any trained zoologist, given the leg of a beetle, can tell

* Prehistoric Rock Pictures, Museum of Modern Art, New York, 1937.

you the name of the bug it belongs to, and no botanist supposes that roses bloom on oak trees. We are familiar with the characteristics of the chemical elements, know how they can be combined, and that in combination they again have different characteristics. We even know what these characteristics are. But what do we know about culture? Nothing. Because we are lazy, phlegmatic and stupid, because we plume ourselves if we can string five or ten citations together to write a witty, anecdotal paper.

2. What do we need, then? Work! And more work! Every fact, object and belief which can help us to understand the growth of human culture should be recorded and indexed for use. It is a pure question of application, first to get the material together and then to see how much we can learn alone from the geographic distribution of certain culture elements.

3. We will find that there are peoples of whom we do not know enough, and so it will be necessary to send out expeditions to find and gather the material we lack.

4. It will be our task to handle our material not only linguistically, descriptively and philologically but also graphically. That means that every expedition will be equipped with a staff of artists who will transfer to paper and canvas that which cannot be recorded accurately with the camera.

5. That is to say, one of the main tasks of a future serious "science of culture" and of a true culture-morphology will be to establish institutions for research and to send out expeditions.

With such singleness of purpose, such honest self-criticism and such complete realization of the practical and intellectual aspects of the job at hand, it was inevitable that Frobenius would carry his enterprise to a successful conclusion.

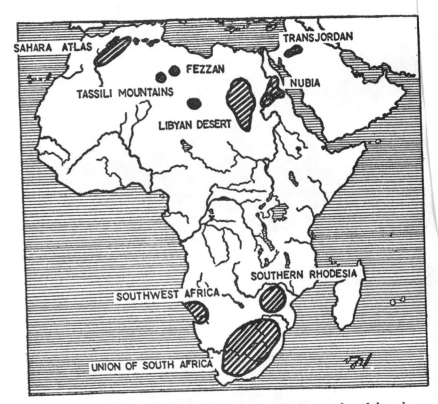

*A Map of the rock-picture areas of Africa explored by the
Frobenius expeditions.*

INTRODUCTION

As pure stories, read for the entertainment they may bring, these tales need no introduction. They speak for themselves. Still, for the more than casual reader who may incline, as we do, to regard them not only as so much narrative but as documents of a very definite ethnological and even of a literary value it may be well to say something of their background.

Putting this material in its geographical and chronological order, we are dealing with a part of the legend and folklore first of the Berbers of Algeria and Morocco, then of the Soninke and the Fulbe of the western Sahel, of the Mande of the Western Sudan, of the Nupe and Haussa of the Central Sudan and of the Wahungwe of Southern Rhodesia.

Beginning at the beginning and taking a long perspective, we may see that out of the dust of the conquests and migrations which in the last two thousand years have swept across North Africa there emerge two peoples, the Arab and the Berber, two peoples beside whom in *that* territory, the Jew, the Turk and the Negro are, culturally, of little importance.

These two peoples are, in many ways, almost diametri-

cal opposites. Each has a different verbal and spiritual
tongue and, though both are Mohammedan, a different
conception of life and living. The Berber, a peasant, is
rooted in the soil. His thoughts do not go beyond his
house, his village or his valley. The Arab, a nomad, pen-
dulates to and fro, carrying merchandise or driving his
flocks of sheep, goats or camels. It is a matter of indifference to him whether he sleeps in the oasis or the town.
The shepherd moves from one grazing area to another.
The merchant travels between his establishments, in two
or more widely separated towns. These are equipped
with wives and other household goods, but are not, psy-
chologically, homes.

The difference between the two forms of thought
becomes apparent when we consider how each views the
mosque. To the Berber the mosque is still the community
house. Here he worships, here he sits in serious council
with his fellows, here his friends spend the night. To him
the mosque is the incorporation of his communal feeling,
it is the altar of his little valley, his community, his home.
To the Arab, on the other hand, the mosque is the symbol
of a binding, world-wide, stereotyped religion, the altar
of an Islam which is everywhere the same.

The Arab knows only one cosmos, *the* cosmos. But
the Berber looks on his home as a microcosm in the macro-
cosm of the universe. While the Berber's conception of
the world is constructive, articulated, full of individual
expression and cosmic mythology, the Arab's is misty
and empty, limited to a borrowed and generalized ideal

and legend (viz: The Arabian Nights), and expresses itself creatively only in the cold monotony of Islam.

None the less the Arab is physically superior to the Berber. The castle-like villages of the latter once rose in every oasis. But, one after the other, they fell before the century long onslaughts of the conqueror from the east till at last the Berber, himself a slave owner, became little more than the Arab's slave. The Arab stormed the oases, took what plunder he could and rode off into the desert. The Berber rebuilt what had been torn down, worked his dates, figs, millet and oil only to have these taken, at harvest time, in another raid. Never able to retain more of his harvest than would keep him alive, he lost interest in his work, let his produce run to seed, neglected his irrigation and did not trouble to fight against the encroaching sand. This is one of the reasons why most of the North African oases are in such sorry shape today.

This repression of the Berber extended geographically from the oasis of Jupiter Ammon (Siwa) in the east to the Atlantic coast of Morocco in the west, the length of the process standing in direct proportion to the ruggedness of the landscape. In flat or desert country suited to the camel, the caravan and its master, the Arab, it was quick; in hilly country slower. The result has been that the old true Berber culture is now preserved only in eastern Morocco (the Riff) and in the Djurdjura Mountains of Algeria, the so-called Kabyl country. In Morocco the Berber has lived for centuries in an Islamic em-

pire. But in the Kabyl country he has remained independent, so independent that even the once powerful
Turk was glad to leave him alone and only the European could conquer him.

The powerful massif of the Djurdjura rises east of
the city of Algiers, its high summit decked with ice and
snow. The torrential streams of its gorges meet in the
Sebau which flows into the sea at Dellis. It is mountain
country in the truest sense of the word and completely
un-African, knows neither palms nor lianas, nor other
tropical growths, but oak, ash and eucalyptus. In the
gardens the vine, the fig tree and the olive sway in green
and silver over the millet and the wheat. The Kabyl, the
master of the vineyard, is the survivor of an ancient
archaistic species and in him we find the essence of the
Berberism which flourished in North Africa before the
Arab came. Its conception of the world, of life and living has been preserved in Kabyl mythology and legend,
handed down from one generation to the next, and of
these legends perhaps none is more direct and charming
for the ethnologist (no matter how earthy the layman
may find them) than that which deals with the creation
of man and the first animals. These legends are of an
archaeological as well as of an ethnological interest, for
they say much of the interesting rock pictures found in
the Sahara Atlas (not to be confused with the High Atlas
of Morocco), a mountain range or series of ranges some
hundreds of miles to the south of the Kabyl country,
ranges not as steep as the Djurdjura and therefore more

accessible to the Arab who soon subdued the local Berber who inhabited them.

Among these pictures, mostly of animals, there is one motif which occurs again and again: that of a man standing with upraised hands before a buffalo or a ram. Curiously the ram and the buffalo never appear together, but

Kasar Amar

Figure 1

each is almost always in combination with a human figure, the group usually forming the center of any number of animal drawings engraved haphazardly around them. Of these rock drawings which are no longer understood by the Arab or the average Berber, those of the buffalo and the ram are the oldest, something which has been established by the patina of the rock, and by the type of stone artifact found in conjunction with them.

Djebel Bes Seba

Figure 2

The Kabyl, who (with one exception) no longer has any memory or knowledge of these pictures, has none the less given us the key to their meaning. His folklore is full of the buffalo and the ram; and the prehistoric connection becomes clearer and clearer as we listen to him talk. We learn how the buffalo Itherther was the king and father of all game animals, how he became lost in the rocky mountains, and how the Kabyl of old used to sacrifice in the bowl from which these animals were born before he set out on the hunt. This, in itself, is a sufficient explanation of the rock picture (which the Kabyl has not seen) of a man standing in worship before a buffalo. Again the stories of the ram who is regarded as the articulator of the year, the one who makes feasts and festivities possible (the story has, of course, been somewhat Islamized), the one who must be consulted about sowing and harvest, make it clear that the ram was the god of agriculture. The exception I mentioned is the weathered engraving of a ram above Häither. Very little of it is to be seen today. But the Kabyl says that before the ram stands a man (and remember that he knows nothing of the Sahara Atlas pictures), a man who "like other men, enquires as to the proper time to sow and reap!"

The stone age buffalo* depicted on the rocks of the

* See figures 1 and 2. Both drawings are cut deep into the rock. They were copied by the painter Carl Arriens on the Frobenius expedition of 1912-1914, retraced in 1934-1935. The natives explain them with the usual words, "hadschra maktuba," (i. e. "writing on the rocks").

Sahara Atlas was the king of the animals and so became
the god of the hunter, and the Sun Ram, * possibly one
of the first of the domestic animals, was the supervisor
of agriculture and is depicted as the god of the peasant.

Thousands of years ago the once flourishing oasis of
Siwa which lies west of Egypt and east of the Djurdjura,
was inhabited almost exclusively by Berbers, who as the
legends indicate, were imbued with the idea of the ram
as the embodiment of a supernatural force. It seems prob-
able that in the course of time this idea filtered through
to Egypt where it was put, so to speak, through the high
powered transformer of the Egyptian *Weltanschauung*
which gave it physical shape so that it returned to Siwa as
the cult of the ram-headed sun god, Jupiter Ammon, the
god whose oracle the great Alexander came to Siwa to
consult. The thought or idea, then, came from the west
and the east gave it form *(hat es gestaltet!)*.

Such are the ideas—they must have seemed old even
to the ancient Egyptians—which still live in the mythology of the Kabyl, ideas which must have once played a
decisive role in North African culture.

From Berber legend we turn to Berber fable. These
are animal stories, some moral, some not—and when
moral, then so in a sometimes devastating but never, as
was too often the case with Aesop, in a consciously ad-
monitory way. The comparison is unfair, for Aesop was
an excellent pedagogue and his tales, as such, have no

* See figures 1 and 2.

equal. The Berber tales are folklore; and in the Berber jackal we meet that shrewd, amusing and unscrupulous spirit always present in peasant lore, whether it be the jackal here, the hare in South Africa (a veritable Brer Rabbit) or the cunning little fox in the Baltic countries (Reinecke Fuchs).

In *Gassire's Lute* we come to legend in its grandest form. The bards who composed the Soninke *Dausi*, of which *Gassire's Lute* is a part, were probably acquainted once with the ancient Kabyls, but the Soninke of today live far far south of the Djurdjura and the Riff.

Between the Sahara in the north and the treed steppes of the Sudan to the south of it, between the Senegal in the west and the Nile in the east, there lies a strip of grassland which would provide scant fare for pampered European stock, but which is considered a fine grazing ground by the Arabs. They call it the Sahel and prefer it to any other part of Africa. In the western part of this region, between the Upper Niger and its tributary the Bani, lies the fertile land of Faraka which is watered—when not flooded—by both of these streams, a watered island in the dry reaches of the Sahel. This, where now the Soninke live, was once a land of the troubadours, a land in which, in the few centuries before and after the beginning of our era, North African chivalry came to flower. In Faraka lived the aristocratic Fasa who had come from the sea and who fought constantly with the Borojogo and the Burdama (the Fulbe and the Tuareg of today).

In the third century A.D. the Fulbe were finally

subdued. This, however, is not the subject of the songs
of the fourth to the twelfth centuries which deal rather
with the heroic period of a much earlier era, apparently
that of the *Garamantenkultur* which Herodotus encountered in the Fezzan and which must have had its high
point at around 500 B. C. The epic story of this culture
or period is contained in what remains of the Soninke
Dausi.

Unfortunately, the culturally destructive influence
of Islam and the increasing tendency to think more of
agriculture than of fighting have made it difficult for
the ethnologist to find more than a scrap or two of the
original *Dausi.* And the scrap given here, *Gassire's Lute,*
is the best part of the epic which has been preserved. In it
we hear repeatedly the four names of Wagadu, the legendary city of the Fasa (men of Fezzan?) : Dierra,
Agada, Ganna, Silla. Dierra is thought to refer to the
place near Mursuk where the ruins of Djerma lie, Agada
to Agadez, north of the Haussa states, while Ganna and
Silla are believed to have been located on the Upper
Niger.

With regard to the fighting which takes place in the
story, I would like to remark that single combat could
occur only between equals, with spear and sword, and
if a hero or any one of the upper casts had to fight with
men of lower standing (in our case the Boroma) he
showed his contempt for them by using only his saddle
girth or a whip. Fighting, like jousting in the Middle
Ages, was a very serious sport. If, as the result of it, one

won a lady of noble birth and a fine mud castle to go with her, then that was as it might be. But the main thing was that one acquitted oneself with honor.

The Rediscovery of Wagadu, which follows, has not the epic quality of *Gassire's Lute,* but rather a Semitic flavor reminding us very forcibly of the story of Jacob and Esau. The stage properties are the same and the derivation of much of it is obvious but the more kindly African turn of the story gives the situation a fitness and a dignity which are lacking in the unvarnished swindle of which we read in Genesis.

The Fight with the Bida Dragon in a somewhat higher key again, gives us human nature at its strongest and weakest. Mamadi Sefe Dekote is willing to wreck a city for Sia Jatta Bari but at the same time Wagana Sako will not challenge his wife's secret lover, for he has heard the man's admission of fear, the Soninke regarding it as un-chivalrous to challenge a man who has admitted that he is afraid.

In *Samba Gana* we have the highest type of chivalry, something which Europeans and Americans are prone to think is characteristic only of the Euramerican cultures instead of something which, like the men of Faraka, we received, in adulterated form, from the Beduin in the first millenium of our era. Chivalry is one of the ear-marks of the proud Hamitic hunting cultures and it still exists today in a very high form among the pure Beduin of the Arabian Desert. Meanwhile it may be of interest to the reader that gigantic tombs of the type built by

Annallja Tu Bari for the hero Samba Gana are still to be found, in varying degrees of preservation, on the Upper Niger today.

In *The Blue-Blood* there is chivalry of a sort which we may or may not admire as well as nationalism of an order not unknown in Europe today. *The Blue-Blood* is a Fulbe tale.

The Fulbe, whom Barth identified with the *Lucae-thiopen*, were, at the beginning of our era, probably a subject people of the Garamantae or Fasa in Central North Africa (the Fezzan). We know from the Silimi-Fulbe in Mossi territory that their ancestors suffered under Fasa rule, while the Bororo-Fulbe in Adamaua speak of their enslavement by the Gara-Fasa of the north and relate how they fled southwards to escape it.

The Gassire legend refers to the "dog-like Boro-ma," the Soninke bards relate how the Boro-jogo could never look a Fasa in the eye and the people of the northern Sahara speak today of the Kel-boro, a subject race which used cattle instead of camels as beasts of burden. These are all references to the ancestors of the Bororo, the present day non-Moslem Fulbe herders of the Central Sudan.

Around the year one, then, the Fulbe were a subject people, primitive and despised. After their migration southwards they fared better and the more adventurous of them lived by the sword just as did the European robber barons in the Dark Ages. In the course of time these emigrants developed an aristocracy and an intense national pride which are well reflected in *The Blue-Blood*.

And, perhaps without knowing that they did so, they adopted the myths and legends of their former rulers as their own, sometimes altering names and minor incidents to suit their purpose, sometimes not even troubling to do that. We need not sneer at them. The legends of Europe are few which have not come, in the very beginning, from Asia; and few "good families" in America or Europe can trace their lineage five hundred years, fewer still a thousand.

And so we have the Mabo, the Fulbe bards, singing the *Baudi* (not to be confused with the Soninke *Dausi*), the epic of the Fulbe heroes, heroes who were sung on the Mediterranean Coast, among the Garamantae (Fasa) in Fezzan and among the peoples of the Sahel and the Sudan long before they were adopted by the suddenly racially and nationally conscious Fulbe.

The Fulbe of today, now in no sense of the word a nation, partly mixed with peasant stock but still largely nomads, are to be found in the Sudan from the headwaters of the Senegal to Kano and then southeastwards as far as the northern reaches of the Cameroons (see map). In the greater part they are fanatic Moslems, the only black fanatics we know in Africa. The non-Moslem Bororo of the Sokoto region, proud of their legendary heroes, are still "heathen."

Leaving the Sahel we go further South to the Sudan proper and there among the Mande we have, in the *Improbable Stories*, that rich humor and delightful exaggeration which are so characteristic of the cheerful, deep-

ly religious, quick-witted, natural and completely charming agriculturalist of the plains, something which we encounter again in a more moral form in the Nupe tales.
The Mande stories are pure negro in spirit, while the
finger-wagging in the Nupe tale, *Gratitude*, makes one
suspect the influence of Islam.

But if there is any moralizing in *The Old Woman* it is
confined to the unheard chuckles of the bard and, I hope,
those of the reader. This is a Haussa tale which is a pane-
gyric on the splendor of African destruction. Old wom-
en, the Haussa say, buy shrewdly in the market but are a
disturbing influence in the home. They are either dried
up, and then their skin is like leather and their hearts
are without blood, or, equally pleasant, they are bloated
beyond all human semblance. In the latter case, their fat
smells and their minds are full of poison. Their hair is
white and bristly. One cannot spin thread from it—at
the most one can twist it into a wiry cord with which
to hang oneself. Their breasts hang long and empty since
their children have sucked all the good that was in them.
And in evil deeds not the devil himself can outdo them.
This is not a pretty picture of feminine old age but, in
the light of the story it is, perhaps, justified. The Haussa,
by the way, live on and four degrees on either side of the
figurative line between Kano and Zinder in what is now
Upper Nigeria.

The myths of Southern Rhodesia are something else
again. In the Berber legends of creation the animals
played the leading roles. In the Wahungwe genesis the

chief character is man and the subject is religion which is to say that it is a statement of man's attitude towards the elemental forces which rule the world he lives in. That his religion often degenerates into magic is obvious in the second to the fifth of the Ngona Horn stories. Religion is the irrational expression of an inner need, magic the rational application of that expression to achieve a material end. Still, there is no point in being pedagogic here. Let us turn to the people themselves.

In Southern Rhodesia on the slopes of Sangano where the Makoni (a Wahungwe people) have their huts today, there lived a king called Madsivoa. Madsivoa's people had a hard life, for they had lost their fire-maker and were forced to eat their meat and fish raw (as do the Abyssinian Amhara today). The fire-maker was not the ethnographic object we know, an instrument of sticks and string, but a horn called moto we ngona, filled with a muschonga (magic) oil and closed with a stopper. If one removed the stopper then the mere fumes from the horn were strong enough to ignite dry tinder. It was the business of the king's daughter and a musarre (priest) to look after the fire-maker. One day, as the result of a quarrel, the musarre hid the fire-maker and died without revealing where it was. Hence the plight of Madsivoa's people.

Legend has it that ngona oil was used to make lightning and in the stories that follow we see that a drop of it was sufficient to make the first woman on earth almost cosmically pregnant and that possession of the horn gave

one magic power over the elements and over game. In
the first story, too, we have the beginnings of a cult (the
identification of the king with the moon, that of his wives
with Venus) which was to result in the sacred state and in
ritual regicide by strangulation, a practice which lasted
till the arrival of the Portuguese.

That the ngona horn itself—with or without magic
properties—is no figment of the imagination can be seen
from the following incident. Among the Wahungwe
Makoni in Rusape there was an interesting tale about
an isolated hill called Chirigwi. There was, it seemed, a
king who wanted the moon as an ornament to hang
around his neck. His people built towers and tried to pile
hills one on the other in order to reach the sky. But the
towers fell and the hills could not be budged. Finally the
king heard about Chirigwi, came there one evening,
climbed to the top and, as the moon rose, broke off first
one horn, then the other. The moon grew new horns
immediately and continued on its way. But the king was
tired. He found a cave on Chirigwi and laid himself to
rest there, one horn to the right of him and one horn to
the left. And then he died. His people took him back to
his own country but they left the horns in the cave. To
be brief, a cave was found and so were the horns (Figure
3) which are now in the possession of the Afrika Archiv,
Frankfurt am Main. They are what the natives call ngona
horns, the thicker one feminine, the other masculine.
They are approximately 35 centimeters long.

Figure 4 is the reproduction of a prehistoric rock en-

graving found in the Fezzan (Central North Sahara).
Two hunters with animal heads are bringing home a
rhinoceros, a feat which, without magic, would be impossible even in the imagination of the prehistoric en-

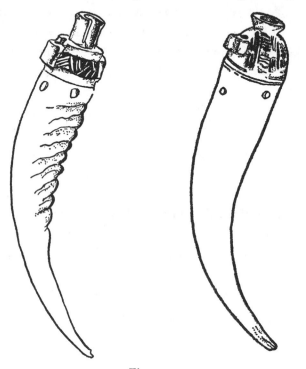

Figure 3

graver. The clue may lie in the horns the hunters carry.
Are these ngona horns or their equivalent? We are not
certain. If they are, then the picture explains itself.

We know that when this picture was made the Sahara
was a comparatively fertile country and we know that
when the slow formation of the desert began the people

who had lived there were gradually forced southwards. We know that some of them reached what is now the South African Union and there are indications that others penetrated into Southern Rhodesia. If these indications are correct it is possible that what we see in figure 4 is the prehistoric representation in North Africa of an idea which, in Southern Rhodesia, has, in legendary form, endured to the present day. At any rate, it is an interesting speculation.

From *Mbila*, the last story in the book, it might appear that the Wahungwe laid little stress on female virtue, for we see that it was impossible to find a virgin princess to sacrifice to Venus so that there might be rain. As a matter of fact, the opposite was true and, except in the case of a princess, it went hard with an unmarried girl who was not a virgin. We know also that when a man married and discovered on the wedding night that his wife was not what she had given herself to be, then he divorced her. The ceremony was a simple one. The next morning the man knocked the bottom out of a jar, gave the jar to his wife and sent her, carrying this expressive symbol, back to her family.

In the royal household matters were otherwise. On the female side the court consisted of the Mazarira, the queen mother, who lived in retirement from the day of her son's accession to the throne, of the Wahosi, the Mambo's (king's) first wife, who reigned supreme, of the Wuabanda, (older women of royal blood) to whom the Wahosi passed on her orders, and of the Wuarango or Mu-

Figure 4

karanga who carried these orders out. The Mukaranga were of good family, usually of royal blood. The king's daughters, the Wasarre (singular Musarre) were also Mukarangas.

In accordance with the cosmic conception on which the state was based, it was thought that there was a connection between the fertility of the royal house and that of the country as a whole. The class upon which it fell to give living and constant proof of this fertility was that of the Mukaranga. And so it happened that the virginity which was virtue in a peasant girl was practically a selfish vice in a Musarre or other member of the Mukaranga class, for if she failed to take advantage of the pleasure that was her right the rains would cease, the crops fail, the cattle die.

And so, in the legend, we need not be surprised that the Wanganga or priests were unable to find a virgin Mukaranga who was likewise a Musarre, particularly in view of the fact that the drought had already lasted a year when the search began. In the course of this year every Musarre who had reached puberty would, very naturally, have done her utmost, through her own sexual activity, to bring an end to the calamity which lay upon the land.

In the course of time it was possible to gather considerable information about rain sacrifices in general and even to learn about a place in the Rusape District at which they were supposed to have taken place. Here on a steep boulder strewn slope, stood a large rock on which

Figure 5

there were a few rock paintings. When members of the expedition had finished copying the pictures they began to excavate the shelter formed by the overhang. Their digging started a landslide. There was a tremendous crash and roar of stone, of enormous rocks and boulders.

Figure 6

The whole valley was filled with dust. Then, when the air cleared and it was possible to get back to work, traces of color were found on a part of the rock which the landslide had exposed. When the spot had been cleaned a picture came to view (Figure 5). The lower part showed a man standing with raised hands before a woman who lay, apparently in sleep, beneath the roots of a tree. It was a picture of the rain ceremony described in *Mbila*, the ceremony supposed to have taken place on the very spot where the picture was found. The picture must have been hidden for a long time for trees were growing in the rubble which had covered it.

In Umbowe, near Sinoya, there was another version of the same story. According to this, the girl was not strangled, but buried alive and when the top of the tree reached the sky a snake crawled out of its branches and sent down the rain. This version may explain the rock painting found later in the Mandarellas District (Figure 6). Incidentally, in Southern Rhodesia as in other parts of South Africa the snake is still and always has been regarded as a symbol for rain.

Douglas C. Fox
New York City
June, 1937

NOTE

THE STORIES in the first and second parts of this book have
appeared in the first, third, sixth, eighth and ninth volumes
of the Atlantis Series of *Volksmärchen und Volksdich-
tungen Afrikas* by Leo Frobenius, published for the Forschungsinstitut für Kulturmorphologie, Frankfurt am
Main by the Eugen Diederichs Verlag, Jena, 1921-1924.
The stories in the third part of this book have been published in Frobenius' *Erythräa*, published by the Forschungsinstitut für Kulturmorphologie, Frankfurt am Main
by the Atlantis Verlag, Berlin and Zurich, 1931. Some of
the Ngona Horn stories have been printed by James
Laughlin.

PART ONE

THE BERBERS

Kabyl Legends of Creation

THE FIRST HUMAN BEINGS, THEIR SONS AND AMAZON DAUGHTERS

In the beginning there were only one man and one woman and they lived not on the earth but beneath it. They were the first people in the world and neither knew that the other was of another sex. One day they both came to the well to drink. The man said: "Let me drink." The woman said: "No, I'll drink first. I was here first." The man tried to push the woman aside. She struck him. They fought. The man smote the woman so that she dropped to the ground. Her clothing fell to one side. Her thighs were naked.

The man saw the woman lying strange and naked before him. He saw that she had a taschunt. He felt that he had a thabuscht. He looked at the taschunt and asked: "What is that for?" The woman said: "That is good." The man lay upon the woman. He lay with the woman eight days.

After nine months the woman bore four daughters. Again, after nine months, she bore four sons. And again four daughters and again four sons. So at last the man and the woman had fifty daughters and fifty sons. The father and the mother did not know what to do with so many children. So they sent them away.

The fifty maidens went off together towards the north. The fifty young men went off together towards the east. After the maidens had been on their way northwards under the earth for a year, they saw a light above them. There was a hole in the earth. The maidens saw the sky above them and cried: "Why stay under the earth when we can climb to the surface where we can see the sky?" The maidens climbed up through the hole and on to the earth.

The fifty youths likewise continued in their own direction under the earth for a year until they, too, came to a place where there was a hole in the crust and they could see the sky above them. The youths looked at the sky and cried: "Why remain under the earth when there is a place from which one can see the sky?" So they climbed through their hole to the surface.

Thereafter the fifty maidens went their way over the earth's surface and the youths went their way and none knew aught of the others.

At that time all trees and plants and stones could speak. The fifty maidens saw the plants and asked them: "Who made you?" And the plants replied: "The earth." The maidens asked the earth, "Who made you?" And the earth replied, "I was already here." During the night the maidens saw the moon and the stars and they cried: "Who made you that you stand so high over us and over the trees? Is it you who give us light? Who are you, great and little stars? Who created you? Or are you, perhaps, the ones who have made everything else?" All the maidens called and shouted. But the moon and the stars were so high that they could not answer.

The youths had wandered into the same region and could hear the fifty maidens shouting. They said to one another: "Surely here are other people like ourselves.

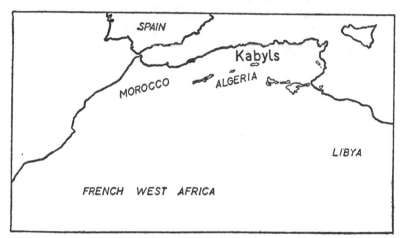

The Kabyl rock-picture area

Let us go and see who they are." And they set off in the direction from which the shouts had come.

But just before they reached the place they came to the bank of a great stream. The stream lay between the fifty maidens and the fifty youths. The youths had, however, never seen a river before, so they shouted. The maidens heard the shouting in the distance and came towards it. The maidens reached the other bank of the river, saw the fifty youths and cried: "Who are you? What are you shouting? Are you human beings, too?" The fifty youths shouted back: "We, too, are human beings. We have

come out of the earth. But what are you yelling about?"
The maidens replied: "We, too, are human beings and
we, too, have come out of the earth. We shouted and
asked the moon and the stars who had made them or if
they had made everything else."

The fifty boys spoke to the river: "You are not like
us," they said. "We cannot grasp you and cannot pass
over you as one can pass over the earth. What are you?
How can one cross over you to the other side?" The
river said: "I am the water. I am for bathing and washing.
I am there to drink. If you want to reach my other shore
go upstream to the shallows. There you can cross over
me."

The fifty youths went upstream, found the shallows
and crossed over to the other shore. The fifty youths
now wished to join the fifty maidens, but the latter cried:
"Do not come too close to us. We won't stand for it. You
go over there and we'll stay here leaving that strip of
steppe between us." So the fifty youths and the fifty
maidens continued on their way, some distance, apart,
but travelling in the same direction.

One day the fifty boys came to a spring. The fifty
maidens also came to a spring. The youths said: "Did not
the river tell us that water was to bathe in? Come, let us
bathe." The fifty youths laid aside their clothing and
stepped down into the water and bathed. The fifty
maidens sat around their spring and saw the youths in
the distance. A bold maiden said, "Come with me and we
shall see what the other human beings are doing." Two

maidens replied, "We'll come with you." All the others refused.

The three maidens crept through the bushes towards the fifty youths. Two of them stopped on the way. Only the bold maiden came, hidden by the bushes, to the very place where the youths were bathing. Through the bushes the maiden looked at the youths who had laid aside their clothing. The youths were naked. The maiden looked at all of them. She saw that they were not like the maidens. She looked at everything carefully. As the youths dressed again the maiden crept away without their having seen her.

The maiden returned to the other maidens who gathered around her and asked: "What have you seen?" The bold maiden replied, "Come, we'll bathe, too, and then I can tell you and show you." The fifty maidens undressed and stepped down into their spring. The bold maiden told them: "The people over there are not as we are. Where our breasts are, they have nothing. Where our taschunt is, they have something else. The hair on their heads is not long like ours, but short. And when one sees them naked one's heart pounds and one wishes to embrace them. When one has seen them naked, one can never forget it." The other maidens replied: "You lie." But the bold maiden said, "Go and see for yourselves and you'll come back feeling as I do." The other maidens replied, "We'll continue on our way."

The fifty maidens continued on their way and so did the fifty youths. But the youths went ahead slowly. The maidens, on the other hand, described a half circle so that they crossed the path of the youths. They camped quite close to one another.

On this day the youths said, "Let us not sleep under the sky any more. Let us build houses." A few of the youths began to make themselves holes in the earth. They slept in the holes. Others made themselves passages and rooms under the earth and slept in them. But a few of the youths said: "What are you doing digging into the earth to make houses? Are there not stones here that we can pile them one upon the other?"

The youths gathered stones and piled them one on the other in layers. When they had built the walls one of them went off and began to fell a tree. But the tree cried and said: "What, you will cut me down? What are you doing? Do you think you are older than I? What do you think to gain by it?" The youth answered: "I am not older than you, nor do I wish to be presumptuous. I simply wish to cut down fifty of you trees and lay the trunks across my house for a roof. Your branches and twigs I will lay within the house to protect them from the wet."

The tree answered: "That is well."

The youth then cut down fifty trees, laid their trunks across his house and covered them with earth. The branches he cut up and stored away inside the house. A few of the larger trunks he set upright in the house to carry the weight of the roof. When the others saw how fine the house was they did even as he had done. Among the youths there was a wild one, just as among the maidens one was wild and untamed. This wild youth would not live in a house. Rather he preferred to creep in and out among the houses of the others seeking someone whom he could rend and devour. For he was so wild that he thought only of killing and eating others.

The fifty maidens were encamped at a distance. Looking, they saw how the fifty youths first dug themselves holes and tunnels in the earth and how they finally built their houses. They asked one another: "What are these other humans doing? What are they doing with the stones and the trees?" The bold maiden said, "I'll go there again. I will sneak over and see what these other humans are doing. I have seen them naked once and I want to see them again."

The bold maiden crawled through the bushes to the houses. She came quite close. Finally she slid into a house. There was no one there. The maiden looked around and saw how fine the house was. The wild one came by outside. He scented the maiden. He roared. The maiden screamed and, dashing out of the house, made for the place where the other maidens were encamped.

All the youths heard the maiden scream and all jumped up and ran after her. The maiden ran through the bushes and screamed. The other maidens heard her. They sprang to their feet and ran in her direction to help her. In the bushes the fifty maidens and the fifty youths came together, each maiden with a youth. They fought in the bushes, the maidens with the youths. Even the wild maiden encountered the wild youth in the bushes.

It was dark in the bushes and they fought in pairs. No pair could see the next one. The fifty maidens were strong. They hurled the fifty youths to the ground, and threw themselves on top of them. And they said to themselves: "Now I will see at last if the bold maiden lied." The maidens seized the youths between the thighs. They found the thabuscht. As they touched it, it swelled and the youths lay quite still. As the maidens felt the thabuscht of the youths, their hearts began to swell. The fifty maidens threw aside their clothes and inserted the thabuscht in their taschunt. The youths lay quite still. The fifty maidens began to ravish the fifty youths. Thereupon the fifty youths became more active than the fifty maidens.

Every youth took a maiden and brought her into his house. They married. In the house the youths said: "It is not right that the woman lies on the man. In the future we shall see to it that the man lies on the woman. In this way we will become your masters." And in the future they slept in the fashion customary among the Kabyls today.

The youths were now much more active than the maidens and all lived happily together in great satisfaction. Only the wild youth and the wild maiden, who had no house, roamed here and there seeking others to devour. The others chased them and when they met them they beat them. The wild ones said to each other: "We must be different from these humans that they treat us so badly. We will do better to keep out of their way.

Let us leave this place and go to the forest." The wild ones left and went to the forest from which, in future, they emerged only to steal children whom they devoured. The wild maiden became the first teriel (witch) and the wild youth the first lion. And they both lived on human flesh. The other young men and women were happy to be rid of the cannibals. They lived happily with one another. Their food consisted only of plants, which they uprooted.

THE BEGINNING OF AGRICULTURE

Meanwhile the first man and the first woman wandered under the earth. One day they found a great pile of millet in a corner. Beside it lay piles of barley and wheat and seeds of all the food plants. A pile of everything lay in a corner. The first man and the first woman looked at the seeds and asked: "What does this mean?" An ant was running along beside the piles of seeds. The first man and the first woman saw the ant. The ant removed a grain of wheat from its husk. The ant ate the grain of wheat. The first man asked: "What is the ant doing?" The woman said: "Kill it! Kill the ugly creature!" The man said: "Why should I kill it? Someone created it just as someone created us." The man did nothing to the ant but watched it instead.

The first man asked the ant: "Tell me what you are doing. Can you tell me anything about the millet and the barley and these other seeds?" The ant said: "I will

ask you something. Do you know of a spring, of a brook
or of a river?" The first man said: "No, we know only
the well." The ant said: "Then you know what water is.
The water is there so that one may wash one's self and
one's clothing. The water is there that one may drink.
It is also there that one may cook one's food. All this
grain is good if one cooks it in water. Now come with
me. I will show you and the first woman everything."
The first man said: "We will come with you."

The ant led the first parents to its hole which led from
under the earth to the earth's surface. The ant said,
"This is my path, come on my path with me." The ant
led the first parents through the passageway and on up to
the surface. The ant led them to a river and said: "Here
flows the water in which you may wash yourselves and
your clothing and which you may drink. This is the
water with which you cook your corn after you have
ground it."

The ant led the first parents to some stones and said:
"These are the stones with which you grind the corn
to meal." The ant showed them how to lay one stone on
the other and how to insert a stick in order to turn the
upper stone. The ant showed them how the grain should
lie between the two stones. The ant said to the first parents: "This is a housemill. With it you must grind the
grain to meal." The ant helped the first human beings to
grind the corn.

The ant showed the first woman how to make dough
with water and meal and how to knead it. The ant said

to the first woman: "Now you must make a fire." The ant took two stones from the river bed and took some dried plants and said: "This is a fire tool." The ant also brought dried grass and wood.

The ant struck a fire with the flint and threw wood and twigs on it. The ant said to the first woman: "When the fire has grown strong and large and has become a heap of glowing ashes you must clear it to one side. On the hot place you must lay your flat cakes of kneaded dough. Then cover them up and throw the hot ashes and the glowing coals over them. After a while the bread will be cooked and you will be able to eat it." The first woman did what the ant had told her. And when she had cleared away the ashes for the second time the bread was done. The first man and the first woman ate the bread and said: "Now we have full stomachs."

The first man said to the woman: "Come, we will take a look at the earth." The first man and the first woman took plenty of barley and wheat with them, and they took the millstones with them and they wandered over the earth. On the way they lost, here and there, a few grains of wheat and barley. Rain fell. The grain which had fallen to the ground took root, grew and bore fruit. The first parents came to the place where the forty-nine young men had built houses and where they lived with the forty-nine maidens as their wives. Till then the forty-nine young men and the forty-nine maidens had eaten only plants which they plucked from the earth. The first parents showed them how to make bread even

as they had learned it from the ant. The forty-nine young
men and women ate their first bread. They told their
parents: "This food is very good. We would like to
accompany you to the place where you found the ant
and the grain in order to fetch some more of it." The first
parents went back with the forty-nine young men and
their wives.

On the way back they saw the wheat and barley which
had sprung up out of the grain which they had lost and
which had fallen to the ground.

They said: "That is the same grain which the ant
showed us how to cook and eat." They grubbed up the
earth and found that each plant had grown up out of a
single grain. They said: "Every grain which fell to the
earth has brought forth twenty to thirty grains. In future we will eat half our grain and put the other half
in the earth."

They threw half of their grain on the earth. But it
was the dry season and the sun burned. The corn didn't
grow. They waited and waited but the corn did not appear. Thereupon, they went to the ant and said: "When
we let a few grains fall for the first time they took root
and grew and each grain produced twenty and thirty
others. Now we have thrown grain on to the earth again,
and not a single stalk has appeared. What is the reason?"
The ant answered: "You have not chosen the right season. After it has been hot for a long time you must wait
till rain has fallen. When the earth is damp then throw in
your corn. And then it will rain again and you will enjoy

a rich harvest. But if you throw your grain on the earth in the hot season it will burn up and you will harvest nothing, for the grain will have been dried up." And the human beings said: "Aha, so one must do it that way!"

Men thereafter did as the ant had taught them. They sowed half their grain after the first rains had fallen. The grain waxed and each stalk bore twentyfold and thirty-fold. And the other half of their grain they ate.

THE FIRST BUFFALO AND THE ORIGIN OF THE GAME ANIMALS

In the beginning there were on the earth a wild buffalo, Itherther, and a female calf, Thamuatz. Both of them came out of the dark space under the earth, the space that is called Tlam. They both came to a river where it flowed out into a valley and there, climbing out of the stream to a rock, they came to the surface of the earth. Before they had known nothing but night and darkness. And as they now climbed up into daylight for the first time they saw the light of the world and they followed it, coming up out of the Tlam and out of the water. Running hither and thither they followed the light of the world. Itherther kept close behind the female calf. He would not part from the female calf. The female calf ran here and there and Itherther followed her.

Itherther and the female calf froze. They felt the cold on their hearts. But they were so happy about the sky and the light that they had no wish to return into the water and into the Tlam. For the world was lighter than anything else and they preferred light to darkness. So they remained in the world.

They ran about, Itherther always behind the female calf. For seven days long the buffalo followed the calf, and they knew not what day and night were. The calf ran ever ahead and the buffalo followed. On the seventh day the female calf pissed. The buffalo looked at the female calf pissing and said: "How is that possible? The calf pisses backwards. But I piss forwards. How is that possible? We must be different." The buffalo pissed, too, and said, "I'm right. Why I can see that I am pissing forwards." The buffalo went to the calf and sniffed her.

On the seventh day Thamuatz and Itherther slept. Thamuatz lay before Itherther. Itherther woke up and sniffed Thamuatz. Itherther excited himself and Thamuatz. Itherther began to lick Thamuatz. When Itherther and Thamuatz had excited themselves in this fashion, Itherther sprang on the female calf and covered her just as a bull covers a cow today. This was repeated many times every day until the calf grew heavy and finally bore a bull calf. When the young bull was a year old he looked at his mother. He sniffed at her and knew desire. But the cow was already heavy again and bore a female calf inside her. And as her son, the little bull, sniffed at her, she shoved him aside, even as the cows do today when they are heavy. She shoved her own son aside and went at him with her horns. The little bull was frightened and ran away.

The little bull ran around for three years till he finally came to the country where the forty-nine young men had built their houses and where they lived with their wives.

They had had children by that time and their children had had children so that a number of villages and small farms lay round about. The people saw the first young bull and began to run after him and to try to catch him. The old men ran to the ant and asked her: "What sort of a creature is this that runs around in the world with horns?" The ant said: "The animal is called Achimi. Achimi is the son of the cow." The people said: "What is that? The son of the cow? There is no cow." The ant answered: "Yes, there is a cow." The people asked, "What is a cow?" The ant said: "It is a female creature just as a woman is a female creature. She has breasts, too. But while a woman has two legs and two arms, a cow has only four legs. The two forelegs are short and the two hindlegs are long. And while the woman has breasts in front, the cow has breasts between the thighs of her hindlegs. The breasts are large. And while a woman has only two breasts and two teats, cows have two breasts and four or six teats. If it has only four then all four are large. If it has six, then four are large and two are small. The flesh of the cow and the ox is good to eat. In time you will find more animals whose flesh you can enjoy."

The people ran after the young bull and tried to catch him. The bull ran around and butted them with its horns.

The ant told the people: "You can catch these animals only before they have horns." But the people kept on trying to catch the bull. The bull got wilder and wilder. He said to himself: "To what sort of a barbarous country have I come? I never found anything like this at home. I will go back to the land of my parents." Thereupon the bull changed his direction and ran back to the country from which he had come. He ran to the country in which his mother had borne him.

On the way to the land of his parents the bull met the ant. The ant told him: "I will explain the world to you. I will tell you everything." The bull asked: "Who are you?" The ant replied: "I have been created just like you. But I know more than you do." The bull asked: "What do you know, then?" The ant said: "Son of the cow, you will live for three or five years, but never more than seven." The bull said: "Don't all animals live longer than that?" The ant answered: "Yes, some animals live longer. There are people who live for a hundred and twenty years, but they have to work. If you do not want to work you can live long like your father, Itherther. But you must be satisfied with poor nourishment and you must be satisfied to remain without shelter in bad weather. You must fight the wild animals in your path and you will have no protection. If you can live in such a fashion, you will live long. But if you go to man you will be beloved above all other creatures. Man will give you food and a house and you will have nothing to fear from the wild animals and bad weather. But you will only live for three, five or seven years, but not longer." The bull replied: "I prefer to live long and without the protection of man. Can you tell me anything else?"

The ant said: "I can tell you that in one thing you are different from all the other animals, that you and all your kind have an advantage which they have not. Go home. In your absence your mother has thrown a calf, a female calf, a Thamuatz. You have what the other animals have not, the right to cover your mother and your sister."

The bull came into the land of his parents. The bull met his mother, the cow. Beside his mother, the cow, was her daughter, the female calf. The young bull ran to his mother and covered her. The young bull ran to his young sister, the female calf, and covered her. But the female calf was young and as soon as the bull had covered her she lay down. For this reason all cows lie down today when bulls have covered them; large and small lie down on the ground when they have been covered.

The buffalo, Itherther, was angry when he saw how the young bull had covered his wife and daughter. He charged the bull. He fought with the young bull, his son. But the young bull, his son, was stronger than he. He threw Itherther, his father, to one side. Itherther fled. He ran into the forest. He kept away from the cows and the bull, his son.

Itherther ran into the stony mountains, among the rocks near Häithar.*

---

* That is a part of the Djurdjura above Mizane in the Beni Burardan territory. It is four or five kilometers from Mizane, high up, and snow

Itherther ran around in the rocks near Häithar. Ali Itherther Mskin was alone. He could not forget the cow. His semen increased inside him. He knew not what to do. One day near Häithar he saw a rock which was flat and had a depression in it. It was like a bowl. When Itherther could not hold himself any longer he went to the bowl and let his semen flow into it. Every time when the thought of the cow hurt him and he could no longer hold himself he let his semen run into the bowl so that it filled. The bowl was almost full. The sun shone with full force on Häithar and the bowl. Ali Itherther Mskin descended into the cool valley. The bowl with Ali Itherther Mskin's semen stood alone in the sun.

Ali Itherther Mskin stayed five months in the valley. Then he came back. He came to Häithar. A male and a female gazelle had arisen from the semen in the bowl. And there were other animals, seven pair in all, always a male and always a female. And all these animals had come from the semen which Ali Itherther Mskin had let fall into the stone bowl.

The animals did not know what to do. Ali Itherther

lies there in winter. The place is called Wuahäithar. The buffalo is worshipped there today as an anthropomorphic being named Ali Itherther Mskin. In the neighborhood are a number of ancient drawings of buffalos and men chiseled into the rock as well as more recent writings in Arabic. There one sees the traces of the anthropomorphic buffalo on the rock. And there, in the rock, is a stone house with a door and a window, really a cave. Only people pure in heart dare go there. And there those who are in trouble make their sacrifices. Sterile mothers sacrifice for children, especially for sons. There one sacrifices when the rain holds off. And there one prays for a good harvest. It is a very holy place and the Kabyls, when they are in the greatest need, always go there.

Mskin fed them with weeds and wild roots. At first the gazelle and other wild creatures were very small and could not run. But Ali Itherther nourished them so well that they could soon run about and seek their own food.

When the seven pair of wild animals were grown, Ali Itherther called them and said: "Each of you is either a male or a female creature. And you must do as I, in my time, did with the cow. If you do this you will have children and multiply." The animals did as he had said and soon they were many. They multiplied more and more and became the creatures which we meet in the forest and on the steppe today.

Only the lion originated otherwise. The lion was once a cannibalistic man (Ihebill). But the cat is a child of the lion. Thus the wild animals arose on the earth.

The bowl in which Itherther let his seed fall is still at Häithar. And in former times the Kabyls sacrificed in it before setting out on the chase.

THE FIRST DOMESTIC CATTLE

Meanwhile the young bull, after he had chased Ali Itherther Mskin away, had often covered his mother and sister and had produced a great number of calves and cows and bulls. The young bull had become a very old bull and out of the three there had come a whole herd. The herd grazed where it would. The herd lived in the wilderness and multiplied.

But one day the first snow fell. It snowed for seven

days and for seven nights. The snow covered all trees and plants. The snow covered the whole earth. When the cows and bulls wanted to lie down they lay in the cold snow. When they wanted to eat they could find nothing for the snow had covered everything. The cows and bulls froze and hungered.

Then the old bull thought of what the ant had said to him in their encounter after he had left man and was on his way back to his parents. The once young and now old bull said: "The ant was right. It is better to have a short life with man, to be beloved and comfortable, than it is to live long and die miserably here in the wilderness." All the cows and bulls froze. The once young, now old bull said: "Come with me and we will go to the land of man. Man will give us food and a warm house. We do not want to freeze and hunger."

The old bull led the herd to the land of man. He scented the warmth and the smoke. The cows and bulls followed him. They came to the villages of man. They ran into the houses. In one house ran three, in another five, in another seven cattle. The people threw them grass and hay. They brought them water. The cows and bulls got warm, ate themselves full and felt fine. Thus came cattle to mankind.

THE FIRST SHEEP AND THE ARTICULATION
OF THE YEAR

One day the first mother of man ground corn with her
handmill, mixed the meal with water and in the hour of
T-ha (between 9 and 9.30 A. M.) she moulded the dough
into the form of a ewe. The hands of the first mother of
mankind were sooty from the cookpots. For that reason
the head of the creature she moulded was black, but the
body, throat and legs were white. She put the sheep of
dough down by the chaff that lay by the millstone. It
was barley chaff. The chaff stuck to the dough animal
and later became wool.

On the next day the first mother of the world made
dough of meal and water and moulded an animal in the
shape of a ram. She gave him horns. But the horns were
not pointed upwards so that he would be able to gore
people with them. She bent the horns and the ears like a
snail, one left and the other right. As she laid the dough
ram in the chaff, there came a sound: "Baa, Baa, Baa."
The little sheep which she had made the day before had
come to life and now bleated out of the chaff. The first
mother of the world said: "What is that? The first sheep
that I made out of dough can make itself heard even as I
can. I'll give it some of my food to eat." Thereupon the
first mother of the world laid the black ram in the chaff
beside the little sheep and gave the young sheep some of
her Kuskus to eat.

On the third day the first mother of the world made

another ewe out of dough, this one quite white. On the
fourth day the mother of the world made another ram.
And he was also quite white. On the fifth day four living
sheep lay in the chaff. One of the ewes had a black head,
but all the rest of her was white. The other ewe was all
white. The other two sheep were rams, one black, one
white. When the first mother of the world had made the
sheep she said to the first father of the world: "That is
enough." After that she made no more sheep.

The first mother of the world kept the four sheep in
her house and fed them. The four sheep grew and bleated.
The people who lived in the neighborhood heard the
bleating. They came and said: "What is that you have in
your house? What makes such a noise?" The first mother
of the world said: "It is nothing. It amounts to nothing.
It is nothing that you have not, too. It is just my bread
yelling." But the first mother of the world gave the sheep
plenty of Kuskus and other foods so that they grew
quickly and became large.

One day, when the sheep were grown up, they ran to
the door. They pushed the door open a little and looked
out. There, in the open air, they saw the grass. They ran
out and began to eat the grass. They ate all the grass
around and began to graze here and there.

The neighbors saw the sheep, came to the first mother
of the world and said: "We have cattle, bulls and cows.
Them we know. But what sort of animals are these?
How have you made these sheep?" The first mother of
the world would not say how she had made the sheep;

she said: "The animals came to me by night. I received
them kindly and they stayed with me. These animals
have been created even as human beings were, even as
you and I."

The neighbors left. They went to the ant and asked
her: "What sort of animals are these? How have they
been created? Who made them? What are they good
for?" The ant said: "These creatures are called sheep
and they should be well cared for by man. They are good
to eat. Their hair is wool from which women can weave
a burnous. They are also for festivals. Without sheep
you cannot celebrate the great festivals. These festivals
are exactly differentiated according to the month of the
year. There are twelve months in the year and every
month has thirty days. Every day has a daytime and a
night-time. In these periods of time the festivals occur."

The people asked: "What festivals are we to celebrate?" The ant said: "One of the festivals is the Lääid
thamthiend (in July). For it one kills cattle and five or
six sheep in every village. Every man who has a wife,
sticks his Debus in the ground (a Debus is a war club)
and when the food is divided he gives his club the same
amount that he himself receives. The second festival is
the Lääid thamkorand (in October). At this festival
every married man must kill a sheep and lay his children
on it so that they will be healthy and strong. A shoulder,
the stomach, an ear and an eye of the slaughtered sheep
must be dried in the sun, laid in salt and then kept for a
month and ten days for the next festival. This third fes-

tival is the Thaschurt in the course of which the dried and
salted parts of the sheep are eaten. This is the feast of
trembling and fear. He who in the first three days of this
period cuts wood, or works in the fields or does any other
kind of work will fall into convulsions and die. The
women must prepare all food for this festival beforehand.
The fourth festival is the Mulud, three months later
(February). Every village shall buy cattle and slaughter
them. Every man shall stick his Debus in the earth and
take for his family the portion that comes to it (the
Debus). All the holy places shall be lit by torches at night
before the big feast. These are the festivals. And now
that you have sheep, you can enjoy them. Therefore you
must take good care of the sheep."

The people asked the ant further: "But how are the
sheep made? How are we going to be able to get sheep
to celebrate the festivals?"

The ant said: "Go and speak with the first mother of
the world. But take care when you buy anything that
you pay for it with the material out of which that which
you will buy is made. Now go and speak with the first
mother of the world."

The people returned to the first mother of the world
and said to her: "Tell us how the sheep were made and
we will give you that out of which you made them." The
first mother of the world said: "Grind barleymeal in
your grindstones, make dough and mould sheep with it.
Lay the dough-sheep in the chaff. That is how I made my
sheep. Perhaps you can do the same."

The people went and tried it. But the first mother of man was a sorceress. She was the only sorceress at that time and the sorceresses who came later could never do what the first mother of the world had done.

Meanwhile the rams covered the ewes which became heavy. Every year each ewe threw two lambs. The sheep multiplied rapidly. The people saw this and came to the first mother of the world and said: "You have made the sheep out of barleymeal. The ant told us to pay for everything with that out of which it is made. So, if you agree, we will give you barley for the sheep." Thus mankind bought sheep with barley from the first mother of the world. And thereafter all people bought what others made better with the stuff of which it was made. For at that time there was no money.

Thus mankind got its sheep and could celebrate its festivals.

The first ram which the mother of the world made did not, like other animals, die. One day he ran high up into the mountains, so high that he bumped his head against the rising sun. The sun seized him and went off with him.

Earlier one could see a picture of the ram just above Häithar. Before it one could see a man asking, like other men, about the right time for planting and harvest. Only a part of this picture is to be seen now, for when the great frost came over the earth he disturbed not only the mother of the world but also the rocks. And every year the frost chips a bit more away from the picture of the first ram.

Kabyl Folk Tales

THE JACKAL AND THE LAMBS

A ewe had two lambs in a grotto which served her as a house. Every day the ewe went to pasture, grazed, then tore up grass and carried it home between her horns. When she reached the grotto she knocked on the door and called: "The jug between the legs (udder) and the hay between the horns!" This sentence was the password. When the young lambs heard it they knew their mother was outside. So then they opened the door and their mother came in carrying the hay between her horns. The ewe often said to the young lambs: "You must never open the door to anyone but me. You can recognize me by what I say and by my voice." The young lambs promised.

One day the ewe came home as usual with the bundle of hay on her horns, knocked on the door of the grotto and called: "The jug between the legs and the hay between the horns." The little lambs opened the door. Nearby in the bush was the jackal. He heard what the ewe said and he saw the lambs and he said to himself: "That would make a nice meal for me. I'll visit those lambs tomorrow."

The next day the jackal went to the grotto, knocked

on the door and called: "The jug between the legs and
the hay between the horns." The two lambs heard his
words and they noticed his voice. They said to each
other: "That is not our mother. We had better not open
the door." They ran to the door and called to the jackal:
"We do not know your voice and we are not going to
open the door." The jackal ran off.

The jackal went to a wise man and said: "What can I
do to have a voice as soft as a ewe's?" The wise man said:
"Go lie on an ant heap. Let the ants run in and out of
your mouth. The ants will eat away part of your throat
so that it will become quite small, like that of a sheep."
The jackal thanked him and left.

The jackal ran to an ant heap. He laid himself on the
ant heap. The ants ran in and out of his mouth and ate
away part of his throat. His throat grew small like that
of a sheep. His voice grew soft. Towards evening the
jackal went again to the grotto where the young lambs
were, knocked on the door and called: "The jug between
the legs and the hay between the horns." The young
lambs heard him. They said to each other: "That is our
mother's voice." They ran to the door. They opened the
door. The jackal entered. He devoured the two young
lambs and then ran off to the forest. When the ewe came
home she found the door open. She found no lambs. She
said: "That must have been the jackal."

The ewe went as usual to the pasture to graze. She
tore up grass and loaded a bundle on her horns. In the
evening she brought home her bundle of hay between

her horns. One day she saw the jackal. Quickly she threw her bundle of hay at the jackal. The jackal lay buried beneath the hay. The ewe laid herself on the hay. Then she called the shepherd. The shepherd came. The ewe said: "Here under this hay lies the jackal who killed my lambs." The shepherd took his crook and beat the jackal to death.

THE LION AND THE MAN

The lioness bore a lion cub. Soon after his birth the cub said: "There is no one who is as strong as I." The lioness said: "No, there are others stronger than you." But the young lion clung to his assumption and repeated continually: "There is no one as strong as I." He grew, he grew into a big, strong lion and always he said: "There is no one as strong as I."

When he was grown the lioness said to him: "You are big now, so go into the forest." The young lion went into the forest. He attacked the other animals and killed them. He even attacked large animals and killed them. He killed an ox. He killed a camel. One day he met a woodcutter in the forest.

The lion approached the woodcutter and said: "There is no one as strong as I. Why, then, have you entered my forest? I shall devour you." The woodcutter had just driven a wedge into a tree trunk, making a deep crack in the wood. The woodcutter said to the lion: "If you are so strong you can help me first to split this tree trunk and then you can eat me at your leisure."

The lion said: "That's fair enough. I want to show you how strong I am." The lion put his paw into the crack in the wood. The woodcutter withdrew his wedge. The two sides of the crack came together and the lion's paw was caught between them. The lion's paw was held as in a vice. The woodcutter took his stick and beat the lion.

The lion asked: "What are you called?" The woodcutter said: "I am called the son of woman." The lion said: "Free me and I swear to you that I shall never devour the sons of women so long as they are brave." The woodcutter refused to free the lion. The lion said: "I will not touch the sons of women so long as they are alive." Thereupon the woodcutter hammered the wedge into the crack so that it reopened. The lion drew out his paw and went home.

The young lion came home limping. The lioness looked at her son and laughed. The lioness said: "Well, what happened?" The young lion said: "The son of woman is stronger than I." The lioness said: "He it is of whom I spoke." The young lion said: "I received many blows." The lioness said: "Did you make a promise?" The young lion said: "I have sworn not to touch the sons of women so long as they are alive." (Actually, not till they are cadavers.)

During the winter the woodcutter herded his sheep near the edge of the forest. One day two lions came out of the forest. They attacked the man, threw him to the ground and wanted to devour him. Out of the forest came the young lion. The young lion touched the man with his paw and asked: "Are you not the son of woman?" The woodcutter said: "Yes, I am the son of woman. I am he whom you wanted to kill last summer. I am he who gave you your freedom." The young lion attacked the two other lions. One of them he killed. The other, however, was stronger than he. Thereupon the woodcutter seized his axe and killed the big lion.

From then on the man and the young lion were good friends. When the lion was hungry the woodcutter gave him a sheep.

THE BEAUTY OF THE PARTRIDGE

The partridge rolled on the floor of the forest till its feathers had a lovely pattern. The partridge pecked at the rocks till its beak was as red as a ruby. The partridge looked up at the sky until its eyes were blue. Then the partridge came down from the mountain. It met a donkey. The donkey said: "You are so beautiful that you must ride on my back." The partridge mounted the donkey and rode down to the plain.

The mounted partridge met the jackal. The jackal looked at the partridge. The jackal asked: "How did you become so beautiful?" The partridge said: "I rolled my feathers on the floor of the forest, I picked at the rock with my beak, I looked into the heavens with my eyes."

The jackal said: "I'm going to do that, too."

The jackal rolled on the floor of the forest and his hair fell out. The jackal struck his muzzle against the rocks and broke his teeth. The jackal climbed a mountain and looked at the sky. The jackal became blind. The jackal descended from the mountain. But because he was blind he did not see a precipice. He fell over the precipice and crashed on the rocks at the bottom. His entrails fell out.

THE ROBIN

Once upon a time there was a very, very large robin which was the Agelith (chieftain) of all the birds. As Agelith the robin one day issued the following order: "In future we will build our nests not in summer, but in winter." The other birds obeyed. All the birds built their nests in winter. The robin built his nest on a cliff beneath an overhanging rock.

One day it hailed. The hail destroyed all the nests. Only the robin's nest, protected by the overhang, was not destroyed. The other birds whose nests had been destroyed flew anxiously here and there. They passed the robin's nest and heard the robin laughing. The other birds asked each other: "What is the robin laughing about?" They asked the robin: "Why do you laugh." The robin said: "Look, I built my nest so that it would be protected. Your nests are destroyed. My nest is untouched."

Thereupon the other birds grew angry. They beat the robin so badly that it became one of the smallest of all the birds. And since then the robin has had nothing to say at all.

THE JACKAL AND THE HEN

A hen and her chicks lived on a high rock. One day the jackal came and called up to her: "Throw me down one of your chicks or I'll climb up there and eat all your chicks and you, too." The hen was afraid and threw him a chick. And the jackal, pleased, took it home with him. For him, it was a perfect situation. He came to the rock every day and called up to the hen: "Throw me down a chick or I'll climb up there and eat all your chicks and you, too." And every day the hen threw him down a chick.

One day the eagle passed that way and asked the hen: "Hen, what have you done with your chicks?" The hen said: "Every day the jackal comes and calls: 'Hen, throw me down one of your chicks or I'll climb up there and eat all your chicks and you, too.' What can I do? So every morning I throw him down a chick." The eagle said: "Listen, hen, don't do that any more. It is not necessary. The jackal cannot climb up there and so you don't have to throw away your chicks to satisfy his greed." The hen said: "I will try to take your advice."

The next morning the jackal came again and said to the hen: "Throw me down one of your chicks or I'll climb up there and eat all your chicks and you, too." The hen said: "Just try it." The jackal tried it. But as soon as he had scrambled half way up the rock his feet slipped out from under him and he fell down to the ground.

The eagle came by. The eagle saw the jackal's exer-

Kabyl rock pictures of the jackal legend

tions and asked: "Jackal, what are you trying to do?" The jackal said: "The hen used to give me a chick every morning. But today she won't and now I'm trying to get what I want by myself." The eagle said: "My dear jackal, if it is chicks you want then I can show you a country where there are so many chicks that not even you and your whole family could eat them all." The jackal said: "Dear eagle, just show me that country right away. For young chicks are our favorite food." The eagle said: "In that case you'll have to climb on my back." The jackal said: "Then come a bit lower."

The eagle flew down. The jackal climbed on the eagle's back. The eagle went into a steep climb and when he had reached a good height he asked the jackal: "Now, jackal, what does the earth look like to you?" The jackal said: "The earth looks green to me. I see green trees and green fields." The eagle climbed steeply and then asked again: "Well, jackal, what does the earth look like now?" The jackal said: "I can no longer see the trees, I can no longer see the fields. The earth is no longer green. It seems to be black."

The eagle said: "Then you are high enough to be able to see thousands of chicks. So pick out your chick for today." The eagle side-slipped and the jackal slid from his back. The jackal fell. The jackal prayed to God: "Let me fall in water or on a pile of straw." But the jackal fell on a rock and died.*

* There is another version to the story in which the eagle carried the jackal in his talons and brought him so high that he could see nothing at

THE JACKAL AND THE LION

One day the lion's foot was sore and he limped. The lion met the jackal and the jackal saw that the lion limped. The jackal said: "Lion, what's the matter with you?" The lion said: "I've got such a sore foot that I cannot put my weight on it and can scarcely walk." The jackal said: "I know a splendid cure for that. Let's go and kill a cow. Then we'll drag the cow into the woods and I'll make you a cowhide bandage that will fix you up in no time." The lion agreed.

The jackal brought the lion to a place where there were many cows. The lion killed one of them and, limping painfully, dragged it into the woods. The lion and the jackal skinned the cow. The jackal said to the lion: "Wouldn't you rather eat first, before I bandage you?" The lion said: "Catching and killing the cow hurt my foot so badly that I've completely lost my appetite."

The jackal said: "Then I'll bandage you right away." He made the lion lie on his back and put his four feet up in the air. Then he threw the damp hide over the four paws, tied the hide around each paw and all four paws together with the sinews of the dead cow. He said to the lion: "Now you had better stay in this position till the bandage dries a bit and is really firm. And after a while

all. Then he let him go. On the way down the jackal addressed his prayer to Sidi Abdel Kader Djilali, a great saint. The jackal fell in a lake, was almost drowned, called upon the saint again and promised to give him a measure of corn if he would save him. The jackal then felt the bottom under his feet, scrambled ashore, shook himself and said: "And now, my Sidi Abdel Kader Djilali, you can go to blazes." And then he ran off.

you'll feel much better." The lion lay with all four feet in the air. Meanwhile the jackal dragged the cow, piece by piece, to his lair.

When the jackal had taken away all the cow meat he said to the other animals: "Go and visit the lion. He has sore feet. I've made him a bandage but I'm going to be busy for the next few days and will not be able to trouble myself about him any longer."

The other animals called on the lion to ask him about his health. They found him in a miserable condition. The cow hide had dried and was as stiff as iron and, with the now chain-like sinews, it held his legs stiffly in the air. The lion could not move. They took pity on the lion.

At that time the hedgehog and the heron were deadly enemies. And as the heron visited the lion he said: "I know a splendid cure for sore feet. That is hedgehog's blood." The lion said: "I'll think about it." After a time the hedgehog came to pay the lion a visit. The lion said: "The heron told me that your blood was the best possible medicine for my sore feet." The hedgehog said: "The heron spoke the truth. Five drops of my blood are quite enough to heal you completely. On the other hand my blood is not the least bit effective if it is not mixed with heron's brains." The lion said: "Will you come again as soon as I'm rid of this bandage and give me some of your blood?" The hedgehog said: "I'll come any day at any hour. You have only to call me." The hedgehog left.

The lion said to the animals. "Now take off this bandage." Many animals came and they all tried to remove the bandage. But it had become much too dry and hard. Then came the partridge. The partridge, flying back and forth, moistened the cow hide with drops of water carried in its beak. The hide became soft. The animals could remove it. The lion said: "Now I'll try the heron's medicine. Call me the heron and the hedgehog." The heron and the hedgehog came. The lion struck off the heron's head and took out the brain. The hedgehog stepped forward, stuck one of his own barbs in his foot so that a few drops of blood appeared. These he gave to the lion. The lion thanked him and the hedgehog went his way.

The lion wanted to revenge himself on the jackal, the jackal who had tied him up so that he couldn't move for eight days. One day he met the jackal in the woods and sprang at him. But the jackal ducked to one side and fled so that the lion got only his tail. The lion looked at the tail in his paw and said: "The tail will enable me to pick out the jackal who hurt me." The lion ordered all the jackals to be summoned. When the jackal heard that he went to his cousins, his relatives and all the other jackals and said: "The lion is looking for a jackal with a long tail. So you must all cut your tails off as I have done. Then, when you go to the lion in the morning you can be sure that, if you are tailless, nothing will happen to you."

All the jackals cut off their tails. The next morning they obeyed the lion's command. All the jackals came to the lion. The lion saw that he was unable to distinguish the jackal whose tail he had from all the other tailless jackals. And so the jackal was saved.

THE JACKAL AND THE FARMER

A farmer plowed with two oxen from morning till eve. One evening a lion came and said, "Give me one of your two oxen or I'll kill you and both of them." The farmer was terrified. He unspanned one of the oxen and gave it to the lion. The lion took it and carried it away. The farmer went home with the remaining ox and bought another one the same evening so that he would be able to plow again in the morning.

The next day the farmer plowed again from morning till eve and when it was evening the lion came again and said: "Farmer, give me one of your two oxen or I'll kill both of them and you into the bargain." Again the farmer gave him an ox. That evening he bought another ox so as to be able to plow again the next day. The next evening the lion came again and demanded still another ox.

The farmer gave the lion an ox every evening. One evening the jackal came by as the farmer was driving his single ox home. The jackal said: "Every morning I see you leave the farmyard with two oxen and every evening I see you coming back with only one. How does that happen?" The farmer answered: "Every evening when I am finished with the day's work the lion comes and demands one of my oxen and threatens to kill me and both oxen if I do not comply with his wish." The jackal said:

"If you promise to give me a sheep I will free you from the lion." The farmer answered: "If you can free me from the lion I will gladly promise you a sheep." The jackal said, "Tomorrow I will call out in a disguised voice from up there on the hill and ask who is speaking with you. Then answer that it is only an Asko (a block of wood to be split). Have a hatchet ready. Have you understood me?" The farmer said: "Certainly, I have understood you."

The next day the farmer took a hatchet with him to the field and plowed as usual with the two oxen from morning till eve. When it was evening the lion came and said: "Farmer, give me an ox or I shall kill both oxen and you as well." When the lion had said that a deep voice spoke from the hill and said: "Farmer, who speaks with you?" The lion was afraid, ducked down and said in a frightened voice: "That is god." But the farmer replied loudly: "It is only an Asko." The voice answered loudly: "Then take your hatchet and split the block of wood." The lion said softly: "But give me only a gentle blow, farmer." Thereat he bowed his head. The farmer gripped his hatchet and struck at the lion's lowered skull with all his force so that he split it and the lion died. The jackal came down from the hill and said: "I have done what I promised. The lion is done away with. Tomorrow I will come again and get the sheep which you have promised me." The farmer said: "You shall have it."

The farmer came home. He said to his wife: "The jackal has freed me from the lion. Now I will give him a ram. I will kill it. Then you pack it up so that I can take it with me to the field tomorrow." The man killed the ram. As his wife was about to pack it up she said: "Why shouldn't we eat the good ram ourselves?" She put the ram into a leather sack. She laid the leather sack in a wicker basket. But she told the house dog to lie down in the basket beside the leather sack. She said to the farmer: "If, perchance, the jackal does not take the ram in the course of the day, then bring it home again. Otherwise the other animals which have not helped you will eat it during the night. Set down the basket in the field just as it is and then let happen what will."

The farmer went to the field. He put the basket down on the field and cried: "Jackal here is your ram." Then he went to his work without bothering himself further about the basket, the ram or the jackal. The jackal, however, came to the basket in order to take out the ram. As he stuck his nose into the basket, up sprang the dog. The jackal ran away from there as quickly as he could. The dog ran after him for a while but when he saw that the jackal was really too fast he gave up and went home. The jackal swore never to help men again.

In the evening the farmer came. He looked into the basket and found the ram still untouched. So he picked up the basket again with the ram in it, brought it home and said: "The jackal has not called for his ram. Now we can eat it ourselves!"

THE BOASTING JACKAL

One day Uschen the jackal said: "I've been fooled once, but it will never happen a second time."

One day the jackal left his house, came to a shepherd and said: "I can outwit you a hundred times, but you can trick me only once." The jackal pounced on a lamb. The shepherd saw it. He came at once. He wished to free the lamb. But Uschen pissed in the lamb's ear with the result that it followed him blindly. The jackal ran away and the lamb followed. The jackal sprang into the forest and the lamb ran into the forest after him. In the forest the jackal turned on the lamb, killed it and carried his meal home.

The next time the shepherd saw the jackal skulking around his flock he covered his sheep with lime. The jackal hung around the flock. When he saw that the shepherd was far away he ran in among the flock and sprang on a sheep. He sprang on the back of a sheep. But as the wool was thickly covered with lime he stuck there and could not free himself. The frightened sheep and the whole flock ran to the house of the shepherd. The shepherd came out. He saw the jackal stuck to the sheep, seized him and struck him hard. After a short time the jackal seemed to be dead. Then the shepherd threw him into a corner of his house.

When the shepherd opened his door the next morning to let his flock out, up sprang the jackal and darted out. From outside he called back: "Didn't I tell you, shepherd, that you could not outwit me? I will still steal many of your lambs." The shepherd said: "Just you wait till the snow falls."

Winter came. The shepherd's children set out traps. The jackal hid himself behind the traps. As soon as a bird was caught in a trap the jackal dug under the fall-stone and hauled out his booty. He took one meal after another from the traps of the shepherd's children.

The shepherd's children found their traps robbed. They told their father. The shepherd said: "Build a big trap near the small one. The robber can be no other than the jackal." Next to a little trap the children built a big one. When the jackal came again to take a bird from a small trap he failed to notice the big trap beside it and as he dug under the small stone to get at his prey the big stone fell on him and he was buried beneath it.

After a while the children came to see about their catch and found the jackal under the large stone. They took the stone away and began to beat the jackal. But the jackal squirmed in his own excrement so that the children were unable to grasp him, except by the tip of his tail. Suddenly he got away.

The shepherd's children looked for the hole which led to the jackal's den. They took two dogs with them to catch the jackal in case his den should have another exit. The dogs stood on guard. Then the children began to dig. They found a nest of five jackals and killed three on the spot. A fourth ran away but was caught and killed by the dogs. The last, in his fear, sprang into a pool of water and was drowned.

PART TWO

THE SUDANESE

Soninke Legends

GASSIRE'S LUTE

Four times Wagadu stood there in all her splendor. Four times Wagadu disappeared and was lost to human sight: once through vanity, once through falsehood, once through greed and once through dissension. Four times Wagadu changed her name. First she was called Dierra, then Agada, then Ganna, then Silla. Four times she turned her face. Once to the north, once to the west, once to the east and once to the south. For Wagadu, whenever men have seen her, has always had four gates: one to the north, one to the west, one to the east and one to the south. Those are the directions whence the strength of Wagadu comes, the strength in which she endures no matter whether she be built of stone, wood and earth or lives but as a shadow in the mind and longing of her children. For really, Wagadu is not of stone, not of wood, not of earth. Wagadu is the strength which lives in the hearts of men and is sometimes visible because eyes see her and ears hear the clash of swords and ring of shields, and is sometimes invisible because the indomitability of men has overtired her, so that she sleeps. Sleep came to Wagadu for the first time through vanity, for the second time through falsehood, for the third time through greed and for the fourth time through dissension. Should Wagadu ever be found for the fourth time, then she will live so forcefully in the minds of men that she will never be lost again, so forcefully that vanity, falsehood, greed and dissension will never be able to harm her.

Hoooh ! Dierra, Agada, Ganna, Silla ! Hoooh ! Fasa !

Every time that the guilt of man caused Wagadu to disappear she won a new beauty which made the splendor of her next appearance still more glorious. Vanity brought the song of the bards which all peoples (of the Sudan) imitate and value today. Falsehood brought a rain of gold and pearls. Greed brought writing as the Burdama still practice it today and which in Wagadu was the business of the women. Dissension will enable the fifth Wagadu to be as enduring as the rain of the south and as the rocks of the Sahara, for every man will then have Wagadu in his heart and every woman a Wagadu in her womb.

Hoooh ! Dierra, Agada, Ganna, Silla ! Hoooh ! Fasa !

Wagadu was lost for the first time through vanity. At that time Wagadu faced north and was called Dierra. Her last king was called Nganamba Fasa. The Fasa were strong. But the Fasa were growing old. Daily they fought against the Burdama and the Boroma. They fought every day and every month. Never was there an end to the fighting. And out of the fighting the strength of the Fasa grew. All Nganamba's men were heroes, all the women were lovely and proud of the strength and the heroism of the men of Wagadu.

All the Fasa who had not fallen in single combat with the Burdama were growing old. Nganamba was very old. Nganamba had a son, Gassire, and he was old enough, for he already had eight grown sons with children of their own. They were all living and Nganamba ruled in his family and reigned as a king over the Fasa and the dog-like Boroma. Nganamba grew so old that Wagadu was lost because of him and the Boroma became slaves again to the Burdama who seized power with the sword. Had Nganamba died earlier would Wagadu then have disappeared for the first time?

Hoooh! Dierra, Agada, Ganna, Silla! Hoooh! Fasa!

Nganamba did not die. A jackal gnawed at Gassire's heart. Daily Gassire asked his heart: "When will Nganamba die? When will Gassire be king?" Every day Gassire watched for the death of his father as a lover watches for the evening star to rise. By day, when Gassire fought as a hero against the Burdama and drove the false Boroma before him with a leather girth, he thought only of the fighting, of his sword, of his shield, of his horse. By night, when he rode with the evening into the city and sat in the circle of men and his sons, Gassire heard how the heroes praised his deeds. But his heart was not in the talking; his heart listened for the strains of Nganamba's breathing; his heart was full of misery and longing.

Gassire's heart was full of longing for the shield of his father, the shield which he could carry only when his father was dead, and also for the sword which he might draw only when he was king. Day by day Gassire's rage and longing grew. Sleep passed him by. Gassire lay, and a jackal gnawed at his heart. Gassire felt the misery climbing into his throat. One night Gassire sprang out of bed, left the house and went to an old wise man, a man who knew more than other people. He entered the wise man's house and asked: "Kiekorro! When will my father, Nganamba, die and leave me his sword and shield?" The old man said: "Ah, Gassire, Nganamba will die; but he will not leave you his sword and shield! You will carry a lute. Shield and sword shall others inherit. But your lute shall cause the loss of Wagadu! Ah, Gassire!" Gassire said: "Kiekorro, you lie! I see that you are not wise. How can Wagadu be lost when her heroes triumph daily? Kiekorro, you are a fool!" The old wise man said: "Ah, Gassire, you cannot believe me. But your path will lead you to the partridges in the fields and you will understand what they say and that will be your way and the way of Wagadu."

Hoooh! Dierra, Agada, Ganna, Silla! Hoooh! Fasa!

The next morning Gassire went with the heroes again to do battle against the Burdama. Gassire was angry. Gassire called to the heroes: "Stay here behind. Today I will battle with the Burdama alone." The heroes stayed behind and Gassire went on alone to do battle with the

Burdama. Gassire hurled his spear. Gassire charged the Burdama. Gassire swung his sword. He struck home to the right, he struck home to the left. Gassire's sword was as a sickle in the wheat. The Burdama were afraid. Shocked, they cried: "That is no Fasa, that is no hero, that is a Damo (a being unknown to the singer himself)." The Burdama turned their horses. The Burdama threw away their spears, each man his two spears, and fled. Gassire called the knights. Gassire said: "Gather the spears." The knights gathered the spears. The knights sang: "The Fasa are heroes. Gassire has always been the Fasa's greatest hero. Gassire has always done great deeds. But today Gassire was greater than Gassire!" Gassire rode into the city and the heroes rode behind him. The heroes sang: "Never before has Wagadu won so many spears as today."

Gassire let the women bathe him. The men gathered. But Gassire did not seat himself in their circle. Gassire went into the fields. Gassire heard the partridges. Gassire went close to them. A partridge sat under a bush and sand: "Hear the *Dausi!* Hear my deeds!" The partridge sang of its battle with the snake. The partridge sang: "All creatures must die, be buried and rot. Kings and heroes die, are buried and rot. I, too, shall die, shall be buried and rot. But the *Dausi*, the song of my battles, shall not die. It shall be sung again and again and shall outlive all kings and heroes. Hoooh, that I might do such deeds! Hoooh, that I may sing the *Dausi!* Wagadu will be lost. But the *Dausi* shall endure and shall live!"

Hoooh ! Dierra, Agada, Ganna, Silla ! Hoooh ! Fasa !

Gassire went to the old wise man. Gassire said: "Kie-korro! I was in the fields. I understood the partridges. The partridge boasted that the song of its deeds would live longer than Wagadu. The partridge sang the *Dausi*. Tell me whether men also know the *Dausi* and whether the *Dausi* can outlive life and death?" The old wise man said: "Gassire, you are hastening to your end. No one can stop you. And since you cannot be a king you shall be a bard. Ah! Gassire. When the kings of the Fasa lived by the sea they were also great heroes and they fought with men who had lutes and sang the *Dausi*. Oft struck the enemy *Dausi* fear into the hearts of the Fasa, who were themselves heroes. But they never sang the *Dausi* because they were of the first rank, of the Horro, and because the *Dausi* was only sung by those of the second rank, of the Diare. The Diare fought not so much as heroes for the sport of the day but as drinkers for the fame of the evening. But you, Gassire, now that you can no longer be the second of the first (i. e. King), shall be the first of the second. And Wagadu will be lost because of it." Gassire said: "Wagadu can go to blazes!"

Hoooh ! Dierra, Agada, Ganna, Silla ! Hoooh ! Fasa !

Gassire went to a smith. Gassire said: "Make me a lute." The smith said: "I will, but the lute will not sing."

Gassire said: "Smith, do your work. The rest is my affair." The smith made the lute. The smith brought the lute to Gassire. Gassire struck on the lute. The lute did not sing. Gassire said: "Look here, the lute does not sing." The smith said: "That's what I told you in the first place." Gassire said: "Well, make it sing." The smith said: "I cannot do anything more about it. The rest is your affair." Gassire said: "What can I do, then?" The smith said: "This is a piece of wood. It cannot sing if it has no heart. You must give it a heart. Carry this piece of wood on your back when you go into battle. The wood must ring with the stroke of your sword. The wood must absorb down dripping blood, blood of your blood, breath of your breath. Your pain must be its pain, your fame its fame. The wood may no longer be like the wood of a tree, but must be penetrated by and be a part of your people. Therefore it must live not only with you but with your sons. Then will the tone that comes from your heart echo in the ear of your son and live on in the people, and your son's life's blood, oozing out of his heart, will run down your body and live on in this piece of wood. But Wagadu will be lost because of it." Gassire said: "Wagadu can go to blazes!"

Hoooh! Dierra, Agada, Ganna, Silla! Hoooh! Fasa!

Gassire called his eight sons. Gassire said: "My sons, today we go to battle. But the strokes of our swords shall echo no longer in the Sahel alone, but shall retain their

ring for the ages. You and I, my sons, will that we live on
and endure before all other heroes in the *Dausi*. My
oldest son, today we two, thou and I, will be the first in
battle!"

Gassire and his eldest son went into the battle ahead
of the heroes. Gassire had thrown the lute over his
shoulder. The Burdama came closer. Gassire and his
eldest son charged. Gassire and his eldest son fought as
the first. Gassire and his eldest son left the other heroes
far behind them. Gassire fought not like a human being,
but rather like a Damo. His eldest son fought not like a
human being, but like a Damo. Gassire came into a tussle
with eight Burdama. The eight Burdama pressed him
hard. His son came to help him and struck four of them
down. But one of the Burdama thrust a spear through his
heart. Gassire's eldest son fell dead from his horse. Gassire was angry. And shouted. The Burdama fled. Gassire dismounted and took the body of his eldest son upon
his back. Then he mounted and rode slowly back to the
other heroes. The eldest son's heart's blood dropped on
the lute which was also hanging on Gassire's back. And
so Gassire, at the head of his heroes, rode into Dierra.

Hoooh! Dierra, Agada, Ganna, Silla! Hoooh! Fasa!

Gassire's eldest son was buried. Dierra mourned. The
urn in which the body crouched was red with blood.
That night Gassire took his lute and struck against the
wood. The lute did not sing. Gassire was angry. He

called his sons. Gassire said to his sons: "Tomorrow we ride against the Burdama."

For seven days Gassire rode with the heroes to battle. Every day one of his sons accompanied him to be the first in the fighting. And on every one of these days Gassire carried the body of one of his sons, over his shoulder and over the lute, back into the city. And thus, on every evening, the blood of one of his sons dripped on to the lute. After the seven days of fighting there was a great mourning in Dierra. All the heroes and all the women wore red and white clothes. The blood of the Boroma (apparently in sacrifice) flowed everywhere. All the women wailed. All the men were angry. Before the eighth day of the fighting all the heroes and the men of Dierra gathered and spoke to Gassire: "Gassire, this shall have an end. We are willing to fight when it is necessary. But you, in your rage, go on fighting without sense or limit. Now go forth from Dierra! A few will join you and accompany you. Take your Boroma and your cattle. The rest of us incline more to life than fame. And while we do not wish to die fameless we have no wish to die for fame alone."

The old wise man said: "Ah, Gassire! Thus will Wagadu be lost today for the first time."

Hoooh! Dierra, Agada, Ganna, Silla! Hoooh! Fasa!

Gassire and his last, his youngest, son, his wives, his friends and his Boroma rode out into the desert. They rode through the Sahel. Many heroes rode with Gassire through the gates of the city. Many turned. A few accompanied Gassire and his youngest son into the Sahara.

They rode far: day and night. They came into the wilderness and in the loneliness they rested. All the heroes and all the women and all the Boroma slept. Gassire's youngest son slept. Gassire was restive. He sat by the fire. He sat there long. Presently he slept. Suddenly he jumped up. Gassire listened. Close beside him Gassire heard a voice. It rang as though it came from himself. Gassire began to tremble. He heard the lute singing. The lute sang the *Dausi.*

When the lute had sung the *Dausi* for the first time, King Nganamba died in the city Dierra; when the lute had sung the *Dausi* for the first time, Gassire's rage melted; Gassire wept. When the lute had sung the *Dausi* for the first time, Wagadu disappeared — for the first time.

Hoooh! Dierra, Agada, Ganna, Silla! Hoooh! Fasa!

Four times Wagadu stood there in all her splendor. Four times Wagadu disappeared and was lost to human sight: once through vanity, once through falsehood, once through greed and once through dissension. Four times Wagadu changed her name. First she was called Dierra, then Agada, then Ganna, then Silla. Four times she turned her face. Once to the north, once to the west, once to the east and once to the south. For Wagadu, whenever men have seen her, has always had four gates:

Two rock paintings of a fight among animal-headed bowmen. This is in a degenerate style with schematized figures, from the Libyan Desert.

one to the north, one to the west, one to the east and one to the south. Those are the directions whence the strength of Wagadu comes, the strength in which she endures no matter whether she be built of stone, wood or earth or lives but as a shadow in the mind and longing of her children. For, really, Wagadu is not of stone, not of wood, not of earth. Wagadu is the strength which lives in the hearts of men and is sometimes visible because eyes see her and ears hear the clash of swords and ring of shields, and is sometimes invisible because the indomitability of men has overtired her, so that she sleeps. Sleep came to Wagadu for the first time through vanity, for the second time through falsehood, for the third time through greed and for the fourth time through dissension. Should Wagadu ever be found for the fourth time, then she will live so forcefully in the minds of men that she will never be lost again, so forcefully that vanity, falsehood, greed and dissension will never be able to harm her.

Hoooh ! Dierra, Agada, Ganna, Silla ! Hoooh ! Fasa !

Every time that the guilt of man caused Wagadu to disappear she won a new beauty which made the splendor of her next appearance still more glorious. Vanity brought the song of the bards which all peoples imitate and value today. Falsehood brought a rain of gold and pearls. Greed brought writing as the Burdama still practice it today and which in Wagadu was the business of the women. Dissension will enable the fifth Wagadu to

be as enduring as the rain of the south and as the rocks
of the Sahara, for every man will then have Wagadu
in his heart and every woman a Wagadu in her womb.

Hoooh ! Dierra, Agada, Ganna, Silla ! Hoooh ! Fasa !

THE REDISCOVERY OF WAGADU

Wagadu disappeared for seven years. No one knew
where she was. Then she was found again. And then
she was lost again and did not reappear for seven hundred and forty years. There was an old King called
Mama Dinga. Mama Dinga said : "If the great war drum,
Tabele, is beaten, Wagadu will be found again." But
Tabele had been stolen by the Djinns, the devils, who
had tied it fast to the sky.

Mama Dinga had an old bondsman with whom he had
been raised. Mama Dinga had seven sons. The six oldest
sons treated the bondsman badly. This the father, blind
with age, did not see. When the bondsman called the
oldest son to a meal with his father the young man gave
the servant a kick as he came into the room and so did
the next five sons. Only the youngest son said "Good
day" to the old bondsman. When they left the room
again the oldest son filled his mouth with water which
he spewed over the old man. The second son sprinkled
the bondsman with the water with which he had washed
his hands, and it was only the youngest son who gave
the old man a good handful of food. Mama Dinga saw
none of these things.

Mama Dinga was blind. He recognized his eldest son by his arm which was hairy and decorated with an iron arm ring. Mama Dinga would stroke the arm experimentally and then sniff his son's gown. Thus he identified his oldest son. As he was going to bed one evening Mama Dinga felt that the time was near for him to die. So he called his bondsman, his old true servant, to him and said: "Summon my eldest son, for I feel that I shall die soon and I wish to tell him that which it is fitting he should know. Tell him to come after midnight." The bondsman went to seek the oldest son. As he entered the oldest son's house and sought to speak with him the young man gave the old servant a kick. That always happened when the old man had anything to do with the six oldest sons. Only the youngest son had always given him food.

Thereupon the old man went to Lagarre, the youngest son, and said: "Couldn't you borrow your eldest brother's gown and arm ring?" Lagarre said: "Yes, I could do that." The old man continued: "Your father is blind. He can no longer see. He identifies your eldest brother by stroking his arm and arm ring and sniffing his gown. Your father will die soon. He sent me to summon his eldest son. But your older brothers have always treated me badly. And so I will bring you to him instead." Thereupon Lagarre slew a goat and skinned it and drew the hide over his arm so that the arm felt as rough and as hairy as his brother's. Then he went to his eldest brother and said: "Lend me your gown and your arm ring. I am

going to see a man who owes me something." The oldest
brother replied: "If you cannot collect your debts without my gown and ring—then take them. Go to my wife
in that house over there and let her give them to you."
Lagarre went there, received the ring and the gown and
put them on. At midnight he met the old bondsman.

The old bondsman led Lagarre to Mama Dinga, the
king, and said: "Here is your oldest son." The old king's
fingers slid over the young man's arm. They felt that
the arm was rough and hairy. They felt the ring. The
old man took hold of the young man's gown and brought
it to his nose. He smelt that it was the gown of his oldest
son. Mama Dinga smiled and said: "It is true." And
Mama Dinga said further: "On the left bank of the stream
stand four great Djalla trees. At the foot of these four
trees lie nine jars. If you wash yourself in these nine jars
and roll yourself in the dirt of the river bank you will
always have plenty of followers. Wash yourself first in
the first eight jars. And then in the ninth. Let the ninth
go at first. But when you have washed yourself finally
in this ninth jar, then you will be able to understand the
language of the Djinns. Then you will know the language of all animals and also of the birds and will be able
to speak with them. And then you can speak with the
Djinns and ask them where the great Tabele, the great
war drum is. The oldest Djinn will tell you, and when
you have the great Tabele, then you will be able to find
Wagadu again." Lagarre left. He went at once to the
river. He found the four Djalla trees. He found the nine

jars. He bathed himself in the jars. And then he understood the speech of the Djinns, of the animals and birds.

Meanwhile, the next day the other sons of Mama
Dinga joined their father for the morning meal. As the
eldest came Mama Dinga asked him: "Have you done
what I told you." The oldest son asked: "What did you
tell me, and when?" Mama Dinga said: "Last night I
let you come to me and I told you something." The oldest
son said : "But I never spoke with you last night." Then
said the old true bondservant to the king: "Last night
you spoke not with your oldest son but rather with your
youngest. You sent me to summon your oldest son, but
instead of calling him I called the youngest one. For
your six first sons always treat me badly. They are worth-
less, and if your oldest son found Wagadu he would
quickly destroy it. So now if you must slay, slay me —
for the blame is mine." Thereupon Mama Dinga said
to his oldest son: "My oldest, you will not be king for
I have just given all that I had to your youngest brother.
So become a wizard and learn how to ask god for rain.
When you can make it rain the people will come to you
and you will have influence."

Meanwhile the Djinns sent the oldest Djinn to Lagarre. The old Djinn said to Lagarre: "In the bush there
is someone seven years older even than I." Lagarre asked:
"Who is that?" The Djinn said: "That is Kuto." * La-

* A white varanus or large lizard which is considered especially holy
even today. During Ramadan the Marabuts try to catch it to make a
magic concoction from its flesh.

garre said: "In which forest is Kuto?" The Djinn showed him the forest.

Lagarre went to the forest. He met Kuto. He could speak with Kuto for he now understood the language of all the animals and even of the birds. He said to Kuto: "Show me my father's Tabele." Kuto asked: "To which people do you belong?" Lagarre said: "I am the son of Dinga." Kuto asked: "What is the name of your father's father?" Lagarre said: "I do not know." Kuto said: "I don't know you, but I know Dinga—I don't know Dinga but I know Kiridjo, Dinga's father. But there is still someone who is seventeen years older even than I." Lagarre said: "Who is that?" Kuto said: "That is Turume, the jackal, who is so old that he has no more teeth." Lagarre asked: "Where is he?" Kuto showed him the forest where Turume was.

Lagarre went with his soldiers to the forest. He met Turume. Turume asked him: "Who are you?" Lagarre said: "I am the son of Dinga." Turume asked: "What is the name of your father's father?" Lagarre said: "I do not know." Turume said: "I do not know you but I know Dinga. I do not know Kiridjo but I do know Kiridjotamani, Kiridjo's father. I am very old but there is still someone who is twenty-seven years older even than I." Lagarre asked: "Who is that?" Turume said: "That is Koliko, the buzzard." Lagarre asked: "Where does Koliko live?" Turume showed him.

Lagarre went with his men to see Koliko. He asked: "Show me the Tabele of my father." Koliko asked:

"Who are you?" Lagarre said: "I am the son of Dinga." Koliko said: "I do not know you but I do know Dinga. I do not know Dinga, but I do know Kiridjo. I do not know Kiridjo, but I do know Kiridjotamani. I know where the Tabele is but I am too weak and too old either to show it to you or to fetch it. As you can see, my feathers have fallen out from age and I cannot even fly away from this branch where I sit." Lagarre asked: "What is to be done?" Koliko said: "You must see to it that I grow strong again. You must bring me a great deal. Stay here with me for seven days. Let a young horse and a young donkey be slain every morning and give me the heart and the liver of both of them. At night and morning you must feed them to me. If you live up to these conditions for seven days I'll have strength again and feathers and will be able to bring you your grandfather's Tabele." Lagarre stayed there for seven days. Every morning he had a young horse and a young donkey killed and he handed the liver and heart of each to Koliko. Morning and night he fed Koliko. The buzzard's strength and feathers grew. He could fly again. He flew to where the Djinns had tied the Tabele to the sky. But he did not have enough strength to break the thongs with which it was tied. He flew back and said to Lagarre: "Three days longer must you slay a horse and a donkey a day and hand me the heart and liver of each, for I am still not strong enough to break the thongs with which the Tabele is tied to the sky. At the end of three days I will be strong enough." For three days more Lagarre slaughtered a horse and a donkey every day. On the third day Koliko was strong enough. He flew to the sky and wrenched off the Tabele. He brought it to Lagarre.

Koliko said to Lagarre: "Return. For two days you may not touch the Tabele, but on the third day you must beat it. Then you will find Wagadu." Lagarre left. For two days he wandered homewards. Then he beat the Tabele and saw Wagadu before his eyes. The Djinns had kept it hidden all that time.

THE FIGHT WITH THE BIDA DRAGON

Koliko had also said to Lagarre: "When you come to Wagadu you will see the great snake, Bida. Bida used to receive ten young maidens every year from your grandfather. And for these ten young maidens he let it rain three times a year. It rained gold." Lagarre asked: "Must I sacrifice ten maidens, too?" Koliko said: "Bida will make a deal with you. He will demand ten young maidens. This you will refuse. Say you will give one maiden; then keep to your word."

Lagarre came to Wagadu. Before the gates of the city lay Bida in seven great coils. Lagarre asked: "Where are you going?" Bida said: "Who is your father?" Lagarre said: "My father is Dinga." Bida said: "Who is your father's father?" Lagarre said: "I do not know him." Bida said: "I do not know you but I know Dinga. I do not know Dinga but I know Kiridjo. I do not know Kiridjo but I know Kiridjotamani. I do not know Kiridjotamani but I know Wagana Sako. Your grandfather gave me ten maidens every year. And for them I let it rain gold three times a year. Will you do as he did?" Lagarre said: "No." Bida asked: "Will you give me nine maidens every year?" Lagarre said: "No." Bida asked: "Will you give me eight maidens every year?" Lagarre said: "No." Bida asked: "Will you give me seven maidens every year?" Lagarre said: "No." Bida asked: "Will you give me six maidens every year?" Lagarre said: "No." Bida asked: "Will you give me five maidens every year?" Lagarre said: "No." Bida asked: "Will you give me four maidens every year?" Lagarre said: "No." Bida asked: "Will you give me three maidens every year?" Lagarre said: "No." Bida asked: "Will you give me two maidens every year?" Lagarre said: "No." Bida asked: "Will you give me one maiden every year?" Lagarre said: "Yes, I will give you one maiden a year if you will let it rain gold three times a year."

Bida said: "Then I will be satisfied with that and will let golden rain fall three times a year over Wagadu."

There were four respected men in Wagadu: Wagana Sako, Dajabe Sise, Damangile (the founder of the Djaora house from which the aristocratic Soninke families trace their descent) and Mamadi Sefe Dekote (Sefe Dekote means "he speaks seldom").

Wagana Sako was unusually jealous. And for this reason he surrounded his court with a mighty wall in which

there was not a single door. The only way to enter the
court was to jump over the wall with the horse, Samba
Ngarranja. Samba Ngarranja was the only horse which
was able to jump over the wall and Wagana Sako guarded
the horse as jealously as he guarded his wife. He never
permitted Samba Ngarranja to cover a mare for he was
afraid that the foal would be as good a jumper as Samba
Ngarranja and that somebody else would be able to
jump over the wall.

Mamadi Sefe Dekote bought himself a mare. He let
Wagana Sako see him shut her up very carefully in his
house. Mamadi Sefe Dekote, who was Wagana Sako's
uncle, one day stole the stallion, Samba Ngarranja, let
him cover his new mare and then secretly returned him
to his stall. Mamadi Sefe Dekote's mare threw a foal that
promised to be just as good a jumper as Samba Ngarranja
and with which Mamadi Sefe Dekote was certain he
could leap over the wall. When the foal was three years
old it was strong enough for the jump.

Then Wagadu went to war. But in the night Mamadi
Sefe Dekote returned secretly to Wagadu on his three
year old stallion. With a mighty leap he cleared the great
wall, tied up his horse in the courtyard and went to
Wagana Sako's wife. He spoke with her, lay down beside her and laid his head in her lap.

In the same night Wagana Sako also left the lines and
rode home to visit his wife. He put Samba Ngarranja at
the wall and was much surprised to find another horse
tied up in his courtyard. He tied up Samba Ngarranja

and then took a good look at the strange horse. Then he heard his wife talking in the house. He placed his weapons against the wall and listened. But Mamadi Sefe Dekote and Wagana Sako's wife spoke but little. A mouse ran along a beam above them. Below it was a cat. The mouse saw the cat and was so terrified that it fell. The cat pounced on the mouse. Mamadi Sefe Dekote seized Wagana Sako's wife by the arm and said: "Look at that! Just look at that!" The woman said: "Yes, I see." Mamadi Sefe Dekote said: "Just as the mouse fears the cat, so do we fear your husband." Wagana Sako, listening outside, heard what was said. And when he heard it he had to go, for the unknown man had said he was afraid of him. (It was considered unchivalrous for a Soninke to challenge a man who admitted that he was afraid.) Wagana Sako retrieved his weapons, mounted his horse, jumped over the wall and returned to the lines. Later Mamadi Sefe Dekote also left the court and joined his companions in the grey of the morning.

Wagana Sako did not know who had visited his wife that night, and Mamadi Sefe Dekote had no idea that Wagana Sako had returned to Wagadu and overheard him. Therefore neither could accuse the other and the day passed without a quarrel. In the evening a singer picked up his lute and sang. Later Wagana Sako reached over to the player, plucked at the strings and sang: "Last night I heard a word and had I not heard it Wagadu would have been destroyed." (Meant is the word "fear".) Mamadi Sefe Dekote also plucked at the strings of the lute and sang: "Had anyone heard what was said last night Wagadu would have been destroyed. But no one heard."

Thereupon the people of Wagadu said: "Let us return to Wagadu. For if, at the beginning of a campaign, people begin to quarrel then the matter can come to no good end." So they all went back to Wagadu.

The people of Wagadu said: "The next firstborn female in Wagadu shall be given to Bida." The next firstborn female was Sia Jatta Bari. Sia Jatta Bari was wondrously lovely. She was the most beautiful maiden in Soninkeland. She was so beautiful that even today when the Soninke and other peoples want to give a girl their highest praise they say: "She is as beautiful as Sia Jatta Bari."

Sia Jatta Bari had a lover and the lover was Mamadi Sefe Dekote. Everyone in Wagadu said: "We do not know if Wagadu will ever again have a maiden so lovely as Sia Jatta Bari." And therefore Mamadi Sefe Dekote was very proud of his beloved. One night Sia Jatta Bari came to sleep with her lover (without, however, permitting him to touch her). Sia Jatta Bari said: "Every friendship in this world must come to an end." Mamadi Sefe Dekote said: "Why do you say that?" Sia Jatta Bari said: "There is no friendship that can last for ever, and I am the one who is to be given to the snake, Bida." Mamadi Sefe Dekote said: "If that happens then Wagadu may rot, for I shall not stand for it." Sia Jatta Bari said: "Do not make a fuss about it. It is so destined and is an old custom to which we must conform. I am destined to be Bida's bride and there is nothing to be done about it."

The next morning Mamadi Sefe Dekote sharpened his sword. He made it as sharp as possible. He laid a grain of barley on the earth and split it with one blow to test the edge of his weapon. Then he returned the sword to its sheath. The people dressed Sia Jatta Bari as if for her wedding, dressed her in jewelry and fine raiment and formed in a long procession to accompany her to the snake. Bida lived in a great deep well to one side of the town. And there the procession took its way. Mamadi Sefe Dekote girded on his sword, mounted his horse and rode with the procession.

Bida was accustomed, when receiving a sacrifice, to stick his head three times out of the well before seizing his victim. As the procession halted at the place of sacrifice, Mamadi Sefe Dekote took his place close to the rim of the well. Thereupon Bida reared his head. The people of Wagadu said to Sia Jatta Bari and Mamadi Sefe Dekote: "It is time to take farewell. Take farewell!" Bida reared his head a second time. The people of Wagadu cried: "Take farewell, part quickly! It is time!" For the third time Bida reared his head over the rim of the well. Whereupon Mamadi Sefe Dekote drew his sword and with one blow cut off the serpent's head. The head flew far and wide through the air and before it came to earth it spoke: "For seven years, seven months and seven days

may Wagadu remain without its golden rain." The head
fell to the ground far, far to the south and from it comes
the gold which is to be found there.

The people of Wagadu heard Bida's curse. They
screamed at Mamadi and closed in on him. But Mamadi
leapt to his horse, pulled Sia up behind him and spurred
off towards Sama-Markala, a town to the north of Segu
on the Niger, where his mother lived. Mamadi Sefe Dekote had a good horse, sired by Samba Ngarranja. The
only horse which could overtake it was Samba Ngarranja himself. Whereupon the people of Wagadu demanded that Wagana Sako give chase, that he overtake
Mamadi and kill him. Wagana Sako leapt to his horse and
pursued his uncle, Mamadi Sefe Dekote.

Wagana Sako quickly caught up with his uncle whose
horse was carrying a double load. He took his spear and
rammed it fast into the ground. Then he said to Mamadi:
"Flee as fast as you can, my uncle, for if the people of
Wagadu overtake you they will surely kill you. I will
not kill you for I am your nephew. Flee to your mother
in Sama." Then he dismounted and pulled at his spear.
After a time the other people of Wagadu arrived. He
said to them: "Help me to pull my spear out of the
ground. I hurled it at Mamadi Sefe Dekote but missed and
then it went so far into the ground that I cannot pull it
out alone." The people helped him to pull out the spear
and sent him off again after Mamadi Sefe Dekote. Wagana soon caught up with his uncle again and once more
rammed his spear into the ground and called: "Flee to

your mother in Sama!" Again he waited for the people of Wagadu to help him withdraw the spear and then for a third time he repeated the performance with his uncle. By the time the people of Wagadu had caught up with him again Mamadi Sefe Dekote had arrived in Sama.

Mamadi's mother came out of the town to meet the riders from Wagadu. She called to Wagana Sako: "Turn back and let my son come to me in peace." Wagana Sako said: "Ask your son if I did not save him so that he could come to you and if he has not me to thank that he is still alive." Mamadi Sefe Dekote said: "I killed Bida to save this maiden whom I will marry. I cut off the snake's head. Ere it fell to earth Bida's head said, 'For seven years, seven months and seven days may Wagadu remain without its golden rain.' And thereupon the people of Wagadu grew angry and sent Wagana Sako on Samba Ngarranja to pursue and kill me. But he protected me. And so I came here with Sia Jatta Bari."

In Wagadu Mamadi Sefe Dekote had been accustomed to give Sia Jatta Bari mutukalle tamu (about 1000 francs) in gold when she left him in the mornings. For three months long she had received mukutalle tamu every morning. But in spite of this she had not given herself to Mamadi Sefe Dekote. But in Sama, where there was no golden snake to make the land rich, these presents stopped. Sia had no more use for Mamadi. Therefore she said to him one morning: "I have a headache. There is only one way to remedy it: cut off one of your little toes and I will wash my forehead with the blood." Ma-

madi loved Sia very much indeed. He cut off one of his
little toes. After a time Sia said: "I still don't feel any
better. The headache will not stop. So cut off your little
finger. If I wash my forehead with its blood then surely
that will help." Mamadi was very much in love with
Sia. So he cut off his finger. Thereupon Sia sent him a
message saying: "I love only people with ten fingers and
ten toes. I do not love people with nine fingers and nine
toes." Mamadi received the message.

When Mamadi heard this he became very angry, so
angry that he fell ill and almost died. He summoned an
old woman. The old woman came and asked: "What
is the matter with you, Mamadi Sefe Dekote?" Mamadi
said: "I am sick with rage, rage at the way in which Sia
Jatta Bari has treated me. For Sia I killed the snake Bida.
For Sia I brought a curse on Wagadu. For Sia I fled from
Wagadu. For Sia I have given out great quantities of gold.
For Sia I cut off my small toe. For Sia I cut off my little
finger. And now Sia sends me a messenger to say, 'I love
only people with ten fingers and ten toes. I do not love
people with nine fingers and nine toes.' And that has
made me ill with rage." The old woman said: "Your case
is not so difficult. Give me your snuff box." Mamadi
thought the old woman wanted to snuff a pinch of tobacco. He handed her the snuff box. The old woman took
it and said: "So that you may see it is not difficult, look
into the box. A moment ago there was tobacco in it.
And now that I have taken it into my hand the tobacco
has turned to gold. And your case is not even as hard as

that. For it is easier to fill Sia with love than your snuff box with gold. Tell me, if I give you a karté cake (that is, butter from the butter tree) can you get Sia to smear the butter on her head?" Mamadi Sefe Dekote said: "Yes, I can do that." Thereupon the old woman prepared a karté cake with Borri (a magic preparation) and gave the completed charm to Mamadi.

In Sama there was a woman who was an excellent hairdresser. This woman was called Kumbadamba. Mamadi summoned her and said: "I will give you mutukalle tamu in gold if you can use this karté in dressing Sia Jatta Bari's hair. Can you do it?" Kumbadamba said: "That's not so hard. Certainly I'll do it." Mamadi gave her the magic karté and left the rest of the affair to her.

One day Sia summoned Kumbadamba and said to her: "Dress my hair." She called to her servant and said: "Go into the house and fetch karté" (This so-called tree butter is in general use for hair dressing.) Kumbadamba said: "That is not necessary as I happen to have plenty of karté with me." Thereupon she set to work. As soon as she had ordered one side of Sia's head and had rubbed in the butter Sia sprang up and said: "Mamadi is calling me." She ran to Mamadi and said: "Did you call me, my big brother?" (Expression of the most tender affection.) Mamadi had not called; it was merely the Borri which was beginning to work. Mamadi said: "No, I did not call you, for I have but nine fingers and nine toes and I know that you love only people with ten fingers and ten toes." Sia returned and let Kumbadamba go on with her hairdressing. When she had ordered the other side of her head and had rubbed in the butter Sia suddenly sprang up and said: "Let me go. Mamadi is calling me." She ran quickly to Mamadi Sefe Dekote and said: "Did you call me, my big brother?" Mamadi had not called; it was merely the Borri which was beginning to work on the other side of her head. Mamadi said: "No, I did not call you, for I have only nine fingers and nine toes and I know that you love only people with ten fingers and ten toes." Sia returned to the hairdresser and let Kumbadamba finish her work. Kumbadamba smoothed her hair, and made good use of the Borrikarté so that Sia jumped up impatiently and said: "Now at last you can let me go. Mamadi is calling me." She ran to Mamadi and asked: "Did you call me, my big brother." Mamadi said: "Yes, I called you. I wanted to tell you to come to me tonight." Sia said: "Tonight I will come to our marriage." Till now Mamadi Sefe Dekote's attempts to possess Sia Jatta Bari had not met with success.

Mamadi went to his courtyard and commanded that his house and bed be put in order. He had a young slave called Blali in whom he had confidence and whom he had entrusted with the care of his good horse. He called Blali and said: "Give me your old gown to put on. But first wash and clean it thoroughly. Then wash yourself and lay yourself in my house and upon my bed. At midnight a woman, Sia, will come to you. Don't speak a word to her. She shall think that I am at her side and she is accustomed that I say little. Hence my name, Sefe Dekote.

Don't speak with her, but make love to her — properly. You must make love to her. If you haven't done so by morning I will simply have you killed. Have you understood?" Blali said: "I'll do it."

In the night came Sia. Mamadi had left his shoes standing by the bed so that she should see them, recognize them and assume that it was he who lay on the bed. She came, recognized the shoes and lay down beside the slave. She said: "Kassunka" (good night). Blali merely mumbled an answer so as not to give himself away. She said: "My big brother, I know that you speak seldom, but speak with me now. I beg you, answer me now." Blali took Sia in his arms.

The next morning Mamadi Sefe Dekote entered the hut in Blali's clothes and called: "Blali!" Blali answered: "Master!" Mamadi said: "Why haven't you groomed my horse this morning instead of sleeping with this disreputable Sia?" Blali said: "If I haven't done my work this morning isn't it sufficient excuse that I was able to sleep with Sia of whom all Wagadu says she is the most beautiful maiden in the land?" Sia lying there on the bed heard his words. Her whole body began to tremble. Trembling she said: "My big brother, you pay back well." Sia, for shame, stayed in the house the whole day long. She did not dare to venture outside. But in the night she crept out and slunk through the shadows to her own house. And there her shame was so great that she died.

That was Mamadi Sefe Dekote's revenge on Sia Jatta Bari.

SAMBA GANA

Annallja Tu Bari was the daughter of a prince who lived near Wagana and everyone thought of her as very beautiful and very wise. Many knights came to seek her hand, but she demanded of each of them something which he was unwilling to undertake. Annallja Tu Bari's father had owned not only the town where she lived but many farm villages as well. One day he quarrelled with a neighboring ruler about the possession of one of these villages. Annallja's father lost the duel which followed and, in consequence, lost the village, too. And this was such a blow to his pride that he died of it. Annallja inherited the town and the land around it, but she demanded of every suitor not only that he win back the lost village but also that he conquer eighty other towns and villages as well. Years passed. No one cared to venture on so warlike an undertaking. Years passed. Annallja remained unmarried but grew lovelier with every year. But she lost all joy in life. Every year she became more lovely and more melancholy. And, following her example, all the knights, bards, smiths and bondsmen of Annallja's land lost their capacity for laughter.

In Faraka there lived a prince called Gana who had a son called Samba Gana. When Samba Gana grew to manhood he followed the custom of his people and, taking two bards and two servants, left the house of his father and set out to seek and fight for land of his own. Samba Gana was young. His tutor was the bard Tararafe, who

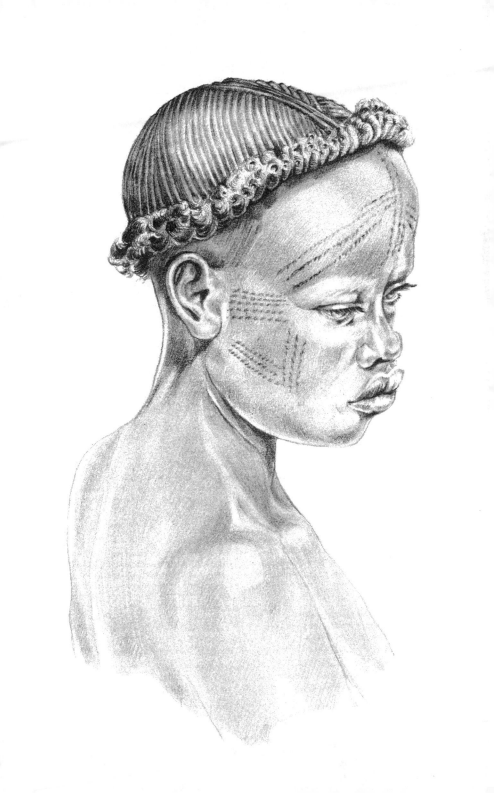

accompanied him. Samba Gana was happy and as he set out on his journey he laughed with joy. Samba Gana came to a town and challenged the prince who ruled it. They fought. The townsfolk watched. Samba Gana won. The conquered prince asked for his life and offered Samba Gana his town. Samba Gana said: "Your town means nothing to me. You may keep it." Samba Gana went on his way. He fought with one prince after another and always he returned the towns which he won. Always he said: "Keep your town. It is nothing to me." Finally Samba Gana had conquered all the princes of Faraka and still he had no town or land of his own for he always gave back what he won and continued, laughing, on his way.

One day he was encamped on the Niger. The bard Tararafe sang of Annallja Tu Bari; he sang of Annallja Tu Bari's beauty and melancholy and loneliness. Tararafe sang: "Only he who conquers eighty towns can win Annallja Tu Bari and make her laugh." Samba Gana listened. Samba Gana sprang to his feet. Samba Gana cried: "Up! Saddle the horses! We ride to the land of Annallja Tu Bari!" Samba Gana rode off with his servants and his bards. They rode day and night. They rode for many days. Finally they came to Annallja Tu Bari's town. Samba Gana saw Annallja Tu Bari. He saw that she was beautiful and that she did not laugh. Samba Gana said: "Annallja Tu Bari, show me the eighty towns." Samba Gana set off once more on conquest. He said to Tararafe: "Stay with Annallja Tu Bari, sing to her, while away the time for her and make her laugh." Tararafe remained with Annallja Tu Bari. He sang every day of the heroes of Faraka, of the cities of Faraka and of the great serpent of the Issa Beer which made the river rise so that one year the people had a surplus of rice and the next year went hungry. Annallja Tu Bari listened to everything he sang. Meanwhile Samba journeyed about the country. He fought with one prince after the other. He conquered every one of the eighty princes. He said to every conquered prince: "Go to Annallja Tu Bari and tell her that your town is hers." All the eighty princes and many knights more came to Annallja Tu Bari and stayed in her town. And so her town grew and grew and presently Annallja Tu Bari ruled over all the princes and knights of the land.

Samba Gana returned to Annallja Tu Bari. He said: "Annallja Tu Bari, all that you wished for is now yours." Annallja Tu Bari said: "You have done your work well. Now take me." Samba Gana said: "Why don't you laugh? I will not marry you until you laugh." Annallja Tu Bari said: "At first I could not laugh because of the pain of my father's shame. Now I cannot laugh because I am hungry." Samba Gana said: "How can I still your hunger?" Annallja Tu Bari said: "Conquer the serpent of the Issa Beer which causes plenty in one year and need in the next." Samba Gana said: "No one has ever dared to attack the serpent, but I will see the matter through." Samba Gana set out to look for the serpent.

Samba Gana rode to Faraka and sought the serpent of

the Issa Beer. He went further and further. He came to Koriume, found no serpent and continued upstream. He came to Bamba, found no serpent and continued further upstream. Then Samba Gana found the serpent. They fought. Sometimes Samba Gana won the upper hand, sometimes the serpent. The Niger flowed first to one side and then to the other. The mountains collapsed and the earth opened in yawning chasms. Eight years long Samba Gana struggled with the serpent. And at the end of eight years victory was finally his. In the course of the fighting he had splintered 800 lances and broken eighty swords. All he had left was one bloody sword and one bloody lance. He gave the blood-stained lance to Tararafe and said : "Go to Annallja Tu Bari, give her the lance, tell her the serpent is conquered and . . . . see if she laughs now."

Tararafe went to Annallja Tu Bari. He said to her what he had been told to say. Annallja Tu Bari said : "Return to Samba Gana and tell him to bring the conquered serpent here so that, as my slave, it may lead the river into my country. Only when Annallja Tu Bari sees Samba Gana with the serpent, only then will Annallja Tu Bari laugh."

Tararafe returned to Faraka with his message. He gave the message to Samba Gana. Samba Gana heard Annallja Tu Bari's words. Samba Gana said : "She asks too much." Samba Gana took up the bloody sword, plunged it into his breast, laughed once more and died. Tararafe drew out the bloody sword, mounted his horse and rode back

to Annallja Tu Bari. Tararafe said: "Here is the sword
of Samba Gana. It is red with the blood of the serpent
and that of Samba Gana. Samba Gana has laughed for
the last time."

Annallja Tu Bari summoned all the princes and all the
knights who were gathered in her town. She mounted
her horse. The knights and the princes mounted their
horses and Annallja Tu Bari rode eastwards with her
people. They rode till they came to Faraka. Annallja Tu
Bari came to Samba Gana's body. Annallja Tu Bari said:
"This hero was greater than all before him. Build him
a tomb to tower over that of every hero and of every
king." The work began. Eight times eight hundred people
excavated the shaft. Eight times eight hundred people
built the underground burial chamber. Eight times eight
hundred people built the sacrificial chamber at ground
level. Eight times eight hundred people brought earth
from afar, piled it on the building, beat it and burned it
to make it hard. The mountain (the tumulus-like pyra-
mid) rose higher and higher.

Every evening Annallja Tu Bari, accompanied by her
princes and knights and bards, climbed to the top of the
mountain and every evening the bards sang songs of the
hero. Every evening Tararafe sang the song of Samba
Gana. Every morning Annallja Tu Bari rose and said:
"The mountain is not yet high enough. Build on until I
can see Wagana." Eight times eight hundred people
carried earth and piled it on the mountain and stamped it
hard and burned it. Eight years long the mountain rose

higher and higher. At the end of eight years, at sunrise, Tararafe looked about him and cried: "Annallja Tu Bari, today I can see Wagana." Annallja peered towards the west. Annallja Tu Bari said: "I see Wagana! Samba Gana's tomb is at last as great as his name deserves."

Annallja Tu Bari laughed.

Annallja Tu Bari laughed and said: "Now leave me, all of you, knights and princes. Go, spread over the world and become heroes like Samba Gana!" Annallja Tu Bari laughed once more and died. She was placed beside Samba Gana in the burial chamber of the mountainous tomb.

The eight times eight hundred princes and Horro rode away, each in a different direction, fought and became great heroes.

Fulbe Legend

THE BLUE-BLOOD

Goroba-Dike was of the blood of the Fulbe house of Ardo which had ruled over Massina for five hundred years. But Goroba-Dike was a younger son and had no landed inheritance. So he wandered around in the Bammana country taking no pains to hide either his dissatisfaction with his fate or the bitterness with which it filled him. If he dismounted at a Bammana village for the night he would order a small child to be slaughtered and ground small, the mince-meat to be mixed with water and the resulting mash to be fed to his horse. If he met a smith he would force the poor man to make him knives and lances without permitting him to use a forge. And when he met a leather worker he would order him to sew up a hippopotamus skull. So, what with one thing and another, the Bammana tribes were thoroughly afraid of Goroba-Dike and of what he might do next.

In their perplexity and their fear the Bammana turned to the Mabo bard Ulal, a wise singer in Goroba-Dike's service. They came with a pot full of gold and said: "You are the only one who can influence Goroba-Dike. We give you this gold that you may tell him that his wildness is only doing the country harm and that neither

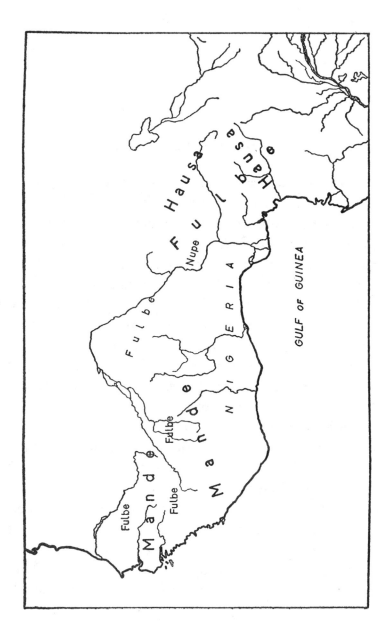

he nor we have anything to gain by it. Try, if you can, to turn him to something else." The Mabo Ulal said: "Good, I'll see what I can do." He took the gold and a few days later he said to Goroba-Dike: "Hear, the Bammana have not injured you in any way. In your place I'd turn my attention to the Pulu, your own people, the people who owe you a kingdom." Goroba-Dike said: "You are right. Where shall we go to first?" The Mabo Ulal said: "How would it be if we were to journey to Sariam where Hamadi Ardo rules?" Goroba-Dike said: "Good. Let us ride."

The two journeyed towards Sariam and dismounted at a peasant's farm not far from the town. Goroba-Dike said to his bard: "You stay here for awhile. I want to take a look at the city by myself." He took off his good clothes, borrowed the peasant's oldest rags and, looking like a beggar, set off towards the town. At a smithy he halted and said: "I am a Pulu and down on my luck. If you give me something to eat I'll be glad to help you with your work." The smith said: "The only thing I can use you for is to work the bellows." Goroba-Dike said: "Gladly." Goroba-Dike went to work with a will.

As he was working Goroba-Dike asked: "To whom does the town really belong?" The smith said: "It belongs to the Hamadi, a twig of the Ardo tree." Goroba-Dike said: "So, to the Hamadi Ardo! Has he horses, then?" The smith said: "Of course. He has many, many horses. He is a very rich man. The town and he are rich, very rich—he has everything he needs. He also has three daughters and two of them have fine brave Fulbe husbands." Goroba-Dike said : "And the third daughter ? She is still a child ?" The smith said : "No, she is not a child. She could even have borne many children by now. But she, Kode Ardo, is the proudest Fulbe maiden in all Massina. On her little finger she wears a silver ring and will marry only him whose little finger this ring fits. For she says that a true Fulbe must have delicate bones and tender fingers. Otherwise he can be no true Fulbe." *

The next morning, as on every morning, all the well bred young Fulbe warriors met in front of Hamadi Ardo's house. They sat or stood and chatted among themselves. Then Kode Ardo, the small proud daughter of the king, came out of the house and among them, drew off her silver ring and sought to find among those present a man whose little finger the ring would fit. One man couldn't even get it over his finger tip, with another it reached the first joint, a third, sweating and straining, brought it as far as the second joint, but no one could slip it properly on his finger. Each would have done so if he could, for all wished to marry Kode. For to possess her was a sign of racial purity. She was the king's daughter. To marry her would bring her husband great esteem.

The following morning the same thing occurred. Again there was no one among all the Fulbe, from

---

* It is a fact that the true Fulbe have an extraordinarily fine and delicate bony structure, something which among Africans as among Europeans is one of the hallmarks of breeding.

far and near, who could slip the ring on his finger. But by this time Hamadi Ardo's patience was at an end and he told his daughter: "Now you must marry the best man at hand." The smith who had given Goroba-Dike employment was among those present and overheard the king's words. He said: "I have a man working for me. His clothes are not exactly clean and he comes from the country. He says that he is a Pulu and one can see he is a Fulbe." Hamadi Ardo said: "Bring me the man. He, too, shall try to slip my daughter's ring on his finger." The smith and a few others ran to the smithy and said to Goroba-Dike: "Come quickly. The king will speak with you." Goroba-Dike said: "What? The king will speak with me? But I cannot go, not in torn and dirty clothes like these." The smith said: "Come, the king commands."

Goroba-Dike went to the big square where the king, where Kode Ardo and all the well-born young men were standing. He went in his ragged clothes. The smith said: "Here he is!" Hamadi Ardo asked him: "Are you a Fulbe?" Goroba-Dike said: "Yes, I am a Fulbe." Hamadi Ardo said: "How are you named?" Goroba-Dike said: "That I will not say." Hamadi Ardo took his daughter's ring and said: "Try to slip this ring on your little finger." Goroba-Dike put the ring on his finger. It fitted perfectly. King Hamadi said: "And *you* must marry my daughter."

Kode Ardo began to weep and said: "I won't marry such an ugly, dirty man, a man from the country." The

king said: "It was your own will. Now you must marry
the man." Kode Ardo wept all day long, but she had to
marry the dirty Goroba-Dike. The marriage was celebrated the same day. That night Goroba-Dike slept with
his wife. The next day Kode Ardo wept. She wept the
whole day and said: "Oh, what a dirty man my father
married me to!"

One morning the Burdama (Tuareg) rode into the
land and stole all King Hamadi Ardo's cattle and all the
cattle of Sariam. The herders came running and said:
"The Burdama have stolen all the cattle. Pursuit! pursuit!" Everyone snatched his weapons. Goroba-Dike
lay idle in a corner. King Hamadi Ardo went to him and
said: "Won't you take horse and ride to war with us?"
Goroba-Dike said: "Climb on a horse? I've never sat
on a horse in my life. I'm a poor man's son. Give me a
donkey. I can stay on a donkey." Kode Ardo wept. Goroba-Dike climbed on a donkey and rode not after the
warriors but in the other direction. Kode Ardo wept and
wept. She said: "Father, Father, what misery you have
brought upon me!"

Goroba-Dike rode to the farmstead where he had left
his horse, his weapons and his bard. He jumped down
from the donkey and said: "Ulal, I have married!" The
Mabo said: "What? You have married? Whom have
you married?" Goroba-Dike said: "I have married the
proudest maiden in the town, Kode Ardo, the daughter
of Hamadi Ardo, the king." The bard said: "What?
You were as lucky as that?" Goroba-Dike said: "Yes.

But today there is something else to attend to. The Bur-dama have stolen my father-in-law's cattle. Now, be quick with my clothes and weapons; saddle me a horse. Then I can take a short-cut across country." Ulal did as he was told and asked: "May I go with you?" Goroba-Dike said: "No, not today." And then he rode off as fast as his horse would carry him.

Soon he overtook the others and rode parallel with them, some distance away. Hamadi Ardo's two sons-in-law and the other Fulbe saw him coming and said: "That must be Djinar, the devil. Let us win him to our cause. Then we'll be victorious and the recovery of the cattle will be assured." A few rode over to him and asked: "Where are you riding? What do you want?" Goroba-Dike said: "I ride to battle and will help him whom it pleases me to help." The men said: "So you are Djinar?" Goroba-Dike said: "Of course, I am Djinar." The men said: "Then will you help us?" Goroba-Dike said: "Why should I not help you? How many of King Ha-madi Ardo's sons-in-law have you in your ranks?" The men said: "Two of them." Goroba-Dike said: "If each of them gives me one of his ears in payment, I will help you." The men said: "But that is impossible! What would people say in the town?" Goroba-Dike said: "That is very simple. All the two sons-in-law need to say is that they lost their ears in battle. They held their heads so — and received only a glancing blow. And that is honorable." The men rode back and reported to the king's two sons-in-law. At first they did not agree but

finally each let an ear be cut off. Then they sent the ears
across to Goroba-Dike. He put the ears in his wallet and
then rode over and put himself at the head of the warriors. He told the Fulbe: "You may not say that Djinar
helped you." The Fulbe said: "No, no, we won't tell."

They met the Burdama. They fought the Burdama.
Goroba-Dike killed more and more and won their horses.
These he gave to the king's sons-in-law. The Fulbe won
the battle. Thereupon they drove the herds of cattle back
towards Sariam. But Goroba-Dike rode off in another
direction and returned to the farmstead where his bard
waited for him. Here he dismounted, laid aside weapons
and clothing, donned the old rags, swung up on the
donkey and rode back to the town. As he rode through
Sariam he was seen by the smith who called to him:
"Keep away from my doorstep. You are no Fulbe. You
are a common, ordinary bastard or a slave, but no Fulbe
warrior." The smith's wife heard him and said: "Stop
your fool talk. A Fulbe is a Fulbe and you're not so very
wise that you could know what there might be behind it."

Meanwhile the victorious Fulbe had arrived with their
recovered cattle. All greeted them with joy. Hamadi
Ardo, the king, even went so far as to approach them.
He said: "That's real fighting. You are still true Fulbe.
Are there any wounded?" One son-in-law said: "As I
attacked from the flank a tall Burdama struck at my head.
I turned my head, the sword took off my ear and I was
saved." The other son-in-law said: "As I attacked on
the other flank a small Burdama struck upwards at my

throat. I nearly had to pay with my head. But I ducked sideways and only lost an ear. The head was saved." King Hamadi Ardo said: "It is a pleasure to hear such things—and you are heroes both. But, tell me, did anyone see my third son-in-law?" Everyone laughed and said: "See him? Why at the very beginning he rode off in the other direction. No, we did not see him."

From the other direction came Goroba-Dike on his donkey. As he drew near he struck the beast and put it to a gallop. When Kode Ardo saw him coming she wept bitterly and said: "Father, Father, what misery you have brought upon me!"

That evening the well-born young Fulbe sat in a circle and told of the deeds of the day. Goroba-Dike lay in his rags in a corner and listened to what was being said. One said: "As I, the first among the enemy, charged . . ." A second said: "When I captured the horses . . ." A third said: "Yes, you are not like Kode Ardo's husband. You are real heroes all." And the two sons-in-law had to relate again and again how they had lost their ears in the heat of battle. Goroba sat nearby and heard everything. His fingers played with the two ears in his wallet. As the night drew on he went into his house. Kode Ardo said to him: "You will not sleep with me any longer. You can sleep on the other side of the room."

The next day the Burdama attacked the town in great numbers. As soon as they appeared on the horizon all the warriors prepared for battle. But Goroba-Dike swung himself up on his donkey and galloped off in the other direction, and the people shouted: "There flees the king's third son-in-law!" Kode Ardo broke into tears and said: "Oh, Father, Father, what misery you have brought upon me!" Goroba-Dike rode to the farmstead where he had left his weapons, his horse and his bard. There he leapt in haste from his donkey and said to Ulal: "Quick, quick, saddle my horse, give me my things! Today there is really something doing. The Burdama are attacking in big numbers and there is no one there to defend the town." The bard Ulal asked: "May I ride with you?" Goroba-Dike said: "No, not today." Then he donned his other clothes, seized his weapons, sprang on his horse and galloped away.

Meanwhile the Burdama had attacked Sariam and surrounded it. One group had broken into the town and was pushing towards the king's kraal. Goroba-Dike, coming from the outside, broke through the ranks. To right and left he hurled men from their saddles, put the spurs to his horse and, leaping over all obstacles, reached his father-in-law's courtyard just as a number of Burdama had seized Kode Ardo and were carrying her off. Kode Ardo, seeing the brave Fulbe coming, called to him: "Big brother, help me, for the Burdama are carrying me off and my cowardly husband has fled!" Goroba-Dike struck down the first man with his spear. From the second he received a gaping wound but struck him down, too. Kode Ardo saw that Goroba-Dike was badly wounded. She cried: "Oh, my big brother, you have saved me, but you are wounded." Quickly she tore off half her gown and wound the cloth around Goroba-Dike's bleeding leg. Then Goroba-Dike spurred his horse once more, sprang into the thick of the Burdama, forcing them to scatter in all directions, running them through and hurling them to the ground and filling the enemy with terror. The Burdama rushed out of the town and set off in desperate flight. The Fulbe pursued them.

Goroba-Dike rode off to the farmstead where his bard Ulal waited. There he dismounted, put aside weapons and clothes and, donning his rags, returned to the city on the donkey. As he passed the smithy the smith yelled: "Look at the bastard, the dog of the street, the coward! Get a move on, you, and get away from my house!" The smith's wife said: "Stop your fool talk. The man's a Fulbe, and one should never abuse a Fulbe." The smith said: "Woman, hold your tongue. One cannot but curse a man who ran away just at the moment when every man was needed." Goroba-Dike said: "What do you expect? Ever since I've been here I've always said I was a poor man's son."

Then he put his whip to the donkey and reached the great square at a gallop. There stood King Hamadi Ardo surrounded by many Fulbe speaking of the events of the day. Kode Ardo stood there, too. When she saw Goroba-Dike riding up with such aplomb she began to weep and said: "Ah, Father, Father, why have you made my life so miserable when there are still such brave and gallant men among the Fulbe." Goroba-Dike answered: "I told your father at the very beginning that I was a poor man's son and understood nothing of horses or fighting." But Kode Ardo wept and said: "Oh, coward, miserable coward! Never shall you share my bed again!" Goroba-Dike, with complete indifference, went over and sat in a shady corner.

Till evening the Fulbe sat around and spoke of the events of the day. One said: "As I repulsed a group of the Burdama . . ." Another said: "As I scattered the Burdama there . . ." A third said: "As I put the main body of the Burdama to flight . . ." But many mocked and asked Kode Ardo: "Where was your husband then?" Kode Ardo said: "Oh, let me be. I had rather my father had married me to an ape than to such a coward. Oh, how ashamed I am!"

It was night. The Fulbe went into their houses. Kode Ardo could not sleep. She thought of her cowardly husband and of the brave stranger who had saved her. At midnight she looked over towards her husband's bed on the other side of the room. She saw that his clothes were in disarray, that the rags had fallen from his body, she saw blood! The blood dripped from a bandage around his thigh, and the bandage was a part of her dress. It was the part of her dress which she herself had torn to bind the wound of the brave Fulbe stranger. And now the bandage was around the thigh of her husband, of the man who had come back on the donkey. Kode Ardo rose, went to her husband and said: "Where did you get that wound?" Goroba-Dike said: "You think it over." Kode Ardo asked: "Who tore off her dress and used it to bind you with?" Goroba-Dike said: "Just think it over." Kode Ardo asked: "Who are you?" Goroba-Dike said: "A king's son." Kode Ardo said: "I thank you."

Goroba-Dike said: "Do not repeat it further for the time being. Now warm up some tree-butter and dress my wound with it." Kode Ardo fetched the butter, warmed it and let it drip on the wound. Then she bandaged the wound. Afterwards she crept out, went to her mother, wept and said: "My husband is no coward — he is no fugitive — he is the man who saved the town from the Burdama today. But do not tell anyone." Then she crept back to her bed.

The next day Goroba-Dike climbed on the donkey and rode back to the farmstead where he had left his Mabo, his horse, his weapons and his clothes. He said to his Mabo: "Today is the day on which we may appear in Sariam in our true colors, the day on which we may pay our respects to the proud Hamadi Ardo. So saddle my horse and yours." Goroba-Dike dressed and took his weapons. He rode into Sariam and his bard followed him. In the great square where all the well-born young Fulbe were gathered he dismounted and his bard drove the hitching pegs into the earth. The pegs were of silver.

Goroba-Dike called his wife. She greeted him and she smiled. Then he turned to the Fulbe and said: "I am Goroba-Dike and this is my wife, Kode Ardo. I am the son of a king and I am he who, yesterday and the day before, put the Burdama to flight." King Hamadi Ardo said: "That I do not believe. We have only seen you riding on a donkey." Goroba-Dike said: "Then ask those who were in the battle." And the men said: "Yes, it is true." Only the king's two sons-in-law said: "It is not certain." Thereupon Goroba-Dike drew the two ears from his wallet and said: "Don't you recognize these ears?" And the two were silent and went away.

King Hamadi Ardo went to Goroba-Dike. He knelt before him and said: "Forgive me. Take my kingdom from my hands." Goroba-Dike said: "King Hamadi Ardo, I am no less than you. For, I, too, am of Ardo blood. And now, if I am king, it is my first order that the smith who insulted me and who is still nothing more than a smith, be given fifty strokes across the buttocks — and with a knotted stick."

And so it came to pass.

Mande Folk Tales

FIVE IMPROBABLE STORIES

1

Three young men went into the bush to harvest millet. It began to rain. The youngest of the three carried a basket full of millet on his head. In the rain his foot slipped, slipped as far as from Bamako to Kati (many, many miles). In falling he reached into a house, picked up a knife, cut the tall reed grass which grew along his path, wove a mat from it and laid the mat under him. In this way the basket of millet on his head spilled on the mat. The young man rose, shook the millet from the mat back into the basket and said: "If I hadn't been quick enough to make this mat and lay it beneath me I'd have had the devil's own job picking up that grain."

The largest of the three young men had forty chickens in a number of baskets. On the way he stopped to let them feed. He took them out of the baskets, strewed millet on the ground and watched while they fed. Suddenly an eagle swooped to grab a chicken. In the same second the young man picked up all forty chickens, put them all in their own baskets, shut the baskets, seized the swooping eagle by the talons and said: "What do you mean by getting fresh with my chickens!"

The medium-sized of the three young men then went hunting with the smallest. The smallest drew his bow at an antelope and let fly. In the same second the medium-sized lad jumped up, ran to the antelope, killed it, skinned and quartered it, laid the hide in the sun to dry and put the meat in his knapsack. Just then the arrow swished through the air. He caught it with one hand and shouted at the smallest lad: "Hey, there! What do you mean by trying to shoot holes in my knapsack!"

2

I saw a woman who gestated for a hundred years. She could not give birth till her son had a long, long beard. The baby ran around inside his mother. He ate, he grew. They circumcised him while he was still inside his mother. But his mother could not give birth to him. One day the baby said inside his mother: "Tomorrow I shall cut off the heads of all the old women in the village." The next morning he was born. He brought a sabre to the world with him and with it he cut off the heads of all the old women in the country.

3

Three young men set out on a journey. One had been turned out by his father because he heard so well. The second had been turned out by his father because he counted so well and the third had been turned out by his father because he saw so well.

The three young men had a sack of millet. They

crossed a river. They loaded the grain on a boat. As they were in midstream the one who heard so well said: "A grain of millet has just fallen into the water. I heard it distinctly." The one who saw so well said: "I'll look for it at once," and jumped overboard. The one who counted so well counted all the grains in the sack of millet and said: "He is right. There is one grain missing." In the same second the young man who saw so well reappeared on the surface of the water and said: "Here it is."

4

Kassa Kena Gananina said: "I am a strong young man. There is no man living who is my equal." He had two comrades, Iri Ba Farra and Kongo Li Ba Jelema. Kassa Kena Gananina had an iron staff. One day he went out in the bush with his iron staff and slew twenty antelopes with a single blow. Then he said to his comrades: "Which of you is going to the forest to gather firewood?" Each was afraid to go alone. Thereupon Kassa Kena Gananina said: "Iri Ba Farra can stay here and keep watch over our meat. Kongo Li Ba Jelema and I will go to fetch firewood." He went off with Kongo Li Ba Jelema.

When they had gone and Iri Ba Farra sat alone there came a big bird, a great big Konoba (kite) who said: "Which shall I take, you or the meat?" Iri Ba Farra said: "You had better take the meat." The Konoba flew off with the meat. Presently the two others returned and Iri Ba Farra said: "While you were gone a big Konoba came and said, 'Which shall I take, you or the meat?'

and I said, 'You had better take the meat.' The Konoba
took the meat and flew off with it." Kassa Kena Gnan-
ina said: "In that case you should have said, 'You had
better take me.'"

The next day Kassa Kena Gananina took Iri Ba Farra
with him to the forest to search for firewood and left
Kongo Li Ba Jelema to look after the meat. When the
two others had gone a big Konoba swooped down and
said: "Which shall I take, you or the meat?" Kongo
Li Ba Jelema said: "You had better take the meat." The
Konoba flew off with the meat. Presently the two others
returned and Kongo Li Ba Jelema said: "While you
were gone a big Konoba came and said, 'Which shall
I take, you or the meat?' and I said, 'You had better take
the meat.' The Konoba took the meat and flew off with
it." Kassa Kena Gananina said: "At least you could have
said, 'You had better take me.' Tomorrow I'll look after
the meat myself."

The next day Iri Ba Farra and Kongo Li Ba Jelema
went to the forest to look for firewood and Kassa Kena
Gananina stayed behind to look after the meat. While
the others were gone a big Konoba swooped down and
said: "Which shall I take, you or the meat?" Kassa
Kena Gananina said: "You shall take neither, neither me
nor the meat." He seized his heavy iron staff and hurled
it at the bird so that it fell dead beside him.

But one of the Konoba's feathers loosed itself from
the bird's wing and floated down on Kassa Kena Gananina's back. It was so heavy that the young man fell to

the ground and, since it was still on his back, he could not rise. Just then a woman came by carrying a small child. Kassa Kena Gananina said: "Call my comrades from the forest that they may lift this feather from my back." The woman went and called the young men in the forest. Both tried to lift the feather, and then they tried together. But they could not move it. The weight of the feather was too much for them.

Then the woman bent over Kassa Kena Gananina, blew gently, blew the feather from his back. Then she picked up the dead bird and gave it to the child she carried to play with. And then she walked off down the road, the child on her back playing with the dead bird.

5

A maiden refused to marry, refused to marry anyone. This came to the ears of a man who liked her. Thereupon he changed himself into a flute and laid himself, in the shape of a flute, before the maiden's door. The maiden found the flute, picked it up, ran to her mother and showed it to her. Her mother said: "What a lovely flute you have. No one in the village has so fine a flute." The maiden took the flute into the house and leaned it against the wall.

In the evening the maiden bathed. Thereupon the flute spoke and said: "I want to bathe, too." The maiden jumped up, ran out of the house to her mother and said: "Mother, the flute just said, 'I want to bathe, too.' Mother, the flute is surely a man." Her mother said: "Don't

bother about it. It is the prettiest flute in the village."
The maiden went back in the house.

The maiden lay down on her bed. The flute said: "I
want to lie down on the bed, too." The maiden jumped
up, ran out of the house to her mother and said: "Mother
the flute just said, 'I want to lie down on the bed, too.'
Mother the flute is surely a man." The mother said: "Forget about it. You have the finest flute in the village. Why
shouldn't you lay it on your bed?" The maiden went
back in her house.

The maiden took the flute from the wall and laid it
beside her on the bed. The flute said: "Oh, but I'd like
to lie between your breasts." The maiden jumped up,
ran out of the house to her mother and said: "Mother,
the flute just said, 'Oh, but I'd like to lie between your
breasts.' Mother, the flute is surely a man." The mother
said: "Oh, don't bother your head about it. You have
the prettiest flute in the village. Why shouldn't you lay
it between your breasts?" The maiden went back in her
house.

The maiden laid herself on her bed and put the flute
between her breasts. Suddenly the flute turned into a
large, strong man with a mighty Fosso which he inserted
in the maiden's Bie. The next morning the maiden went
to her mother and said: "Now I'm married after all, for
the flute was naturally a man. But I'm glad." Her mother
said: "Didn't I tell you?"

Nupe Folk Tales

THE TALKING SKULL

A hunter goes into the bush. He finds an old human skull. The hunter says: "What brought you here?" The skull answers: "Talking brought me here." The hunter runs off. He runs to the king. He tells the king: "I found a dry human skull in the bush. It asks you how its father and mother are."

The king says: "Never since my mother bore me have I heard that a dead skull can speak." The king summons the Alkali, the Saba and the Degi and asks them if they have ever heard the like. None of the wise men has heard the like and they decide to send a guard out with the hunter into the bush to find out if his story is true and, if so, to learn the reason for it. The guard accompany the hunter into the bush with the order to kill him on the spot should he have lied. The guard and the hunter come to the skull. The hunter addresses the skull: "Skull, speak." The skull is silent. The hunter asks as before: "What brought you here?" The skull does not answer. The whole day long the hunter begs the skull to speak, but it does not answer. In the evening the guard tell the hunter to make the skull speak and when he cannot they kill him in accordance with the king's command. When the guard are gone the skull opens its jaws and asks the dead hunter's head: "What brought you here?" The dead hunter's head replies: "Talking brought me here!"

QUESTION AND ANSWER

A father told his son: "If you ever sleep with a maiden you will die." The father hid his son in the bush. He let him grow up in the bush. One day a maiden came out in the bush. The boy saw the maiden. The maiden said: "You live so alone here. Tomorrow I'll come to visit you again." The young man said: "Yes, do come again. I must sleep with you even though my father told me that I would die if ever I slept with a maiden." The maiden said: "In that case I will not come again, for it is not my wish that you should die." The young man said: "No, please, please, come again. I beg you, I beg you, come again!" The maiden said: "Good, I go but I will come again. And if you die, then I will bring you to life again." The next day the maiden came again. The young man slept with the maiden. The young man died. His parents wept. But the maiden ran into the forest to the hunter and told him what had happened. The hunter said: "Why that is nothing at all. All I need is a lizard." The hunter came with the lizard. He built a big wood pile, lighted it, threw the lizard into the flames and said: "If the lizard burns on the funeral pyre the young man will stay dead. But if some one rescues it the young man will come to life again." The father tried to pull the lizard out of the fire. But the fire was hot and large. The mother tried, but she failed, too. But the maiden jumped into the fire, picked up the lizard and brought it out alive. The young man came to life again.

The hunter said: "The young man has come to life again. And now, if he kills the lizard, his mother will die, but if he lets the lizard live, the maiden will die."

The question is: What would a true Nupe lad do?

The answer is: He would kill the lizard at once.

GRATITUDE

A hunter went out in the bush. He met an antelope. He killed the antelope. Boaji (the civet) passed by. Boaji said: "Give me some of that meat. I am hungry. I beg you for it. I'll do you a favor some other time." The hunter gave Boaji some of the antelope's meat. Boaji ran off.

The next day the hunter went out in the bush again. He came to a place where the bush was overgrown and it was hard to see where one was going. There, in the middle of the bush, he met a crocodile. The hunter said: "How did you get here? Don't you belong in the water?" The crocodile said: "Last night I went out hunting and now I am far from the river. I cannot find my way back. I beg you, show me the way to the river. If you do I'll give you five loads of fish." The hunter said: "I'll do that gladly." The hunter tied a thong around the crocodile's foot and led him to the Niger. At the water's edge the

crocodile said: "Now undo the thong and I'll go into
the water and fetch you your five loads of fish." The
hunter freed the crocodile, the crocodile went into the
water and the hunter waited on the bank.

The crocodile came out of the water with a great big
fish and laid it high on the bank. The crocodile slipped
back into the water. The crocodile returned with a second load of fish and laid it lower on the bank. The hunter
climbed down and carried it higher. The crocodile returned with a third load which he left at the water's edge.
The hunter carried the third load up the river bank. The
crocodile brought a fourth load and laid it in the shallows. The hunter came down, picked the fish out of the
shallows and carried it high up the bank. The crocodile
returned with a fifth load of fish which it laid on the edge
of the deep water. The hunter came down from the
bank, waded through the shallows and came to the edge
of the deep water. As he was about to pick up the fish
the crocodile snapped at his foot, caught it fast and
dragged the hunter under the water.

The crocodile brought the hunter to his brother crocodiles who lay on a sandbank in midstream. The crocodile
called all his friends and said: "We have caught a hunter.
We are going to eat him. Come, all of you." The crocodiles came from every side and swarmed around the
hunter. The hunter said: "Is that fair? This crocodile
lost his way in the bush. I brought him back to the river.
And now he wants to eat me." The crocodiles said: "We
will ask four other people what they think about it."

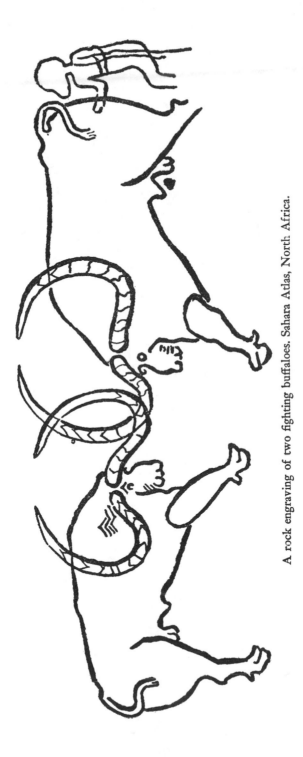

A rock engraving of two fighting buffaloes. Sahara Atlas, North Africa.

Down the river floated an Asubi (colored, oval mat woven by the Benue in the Kutigi region). The Asubi was old and torn. The hunter cried: "Asubi, help me!" The Asubi said: "What is the matter?" The hunter said: "This crocodile here was lost in the bush and I brought him back to the river. I saved his life and now he wants to take mine. Is that fair?" The Asubi said: "You are a man. I know men. When a mat is young and useful, they keep it clean, do not step on it with their feet, roll it up when they have used it and lay it carefully to one side. But when a mat is old they forget what it used to be like. They throw it away. They throw it into the river. The crocodile will do well if he treats you as men have treated me." The Asubi drifted on. The crocodile said: "Did you hear what the Asubi said?"

A dress, old, torn and worn, came floating down the stream. Someone had thrown it away. The hunter cried: "Dress, help me!" The old dress said: "What is the matter?" The hunter said: "I brought this crocodile here, who had lost his way, back to the river. And now he wants to eat me. I saved his life and now he wants to rob me of mine. Is that fair?" The dress said: "You are a man. I know men. So long as a dress is young and beautiful they wear it everywhere, accept its beauty for their own and say, 'Aren't we lovely?' But it is the dress which is lovely. And the people know that they lie for they fold the dress carefully, smooth out the wrinkles and wrap it up. But as soon as the dress is old they forget what it used to be before. They throw it in the river. The crocodile will do well if he treats you as men have treated me." The old dress drifted on downstream.

The crocodile said: "Did you hear what the old dress said?"

An old mare came down to the river to drink. The mare was old and thin. Her masters had turned her out because she was no longer of any use to them. The hunter cried: "O mare, help me!" The old mare said: "What is the matter?" The hunter said: "I brought this crocodile here, who had lost his way, back to the river. Now he wants to eat me. I saved his life and now he wants to rob me of mine. Is that fair?" The old mare said: "You are a man. I know men. When a mare is young they build a stall for her. They send out boys to cut her the best grass. They give her the best grain and when she is in foal they give her double of everything. But when a mare is old and cannot foal, when she is weak and ill they drive her out into the bush and say, 'Take care of yourself as best you can.' Just look at me. The crocodile will do well if he treats you as men have treated me." The mare trotted off. The crocodile said to the hunter: "You heard what the old mare said?"

Boaji came down to the bank of the Niger to drink. It was the Boaji whom the hunter had helped the day before. The hunter cried: "Boaji, help me!" Boaji said: "What is the matter?" The hunter said: "I brought this crocodile here, who had lost his way in the bush, back to the river. And now he wants to eat me. I saved his life and now he wants to rob me of mine. Is that fair?" Boaji said: "That is difficult to decide. First I must know everything. I do not want to hear only your side of the story but the crocodile's side too, — that is, if the crocodile is willing to accept my decision." The crocodile said: "I will tell you." Boaji said: "How did the hunter bring you here?" The crocodile said: "He tied a thong around my foot and dragged me after him." Boaji said: "Did it hurt?" The crocodile said: "Yes, it hurt." The hunter said: "That is not possible." Boaji said: "I cannot decide that until I have seen it. Come ashore here and show me what you did." The crocodile and the hunter went to the shore. Boaji said to the hunter: "Now tie the thong around his foot, just as you did before, so that I can judge whether it hurt him or not." The hunter bound the thong around the crocodile's foot. Boaji said: "Was it like that?" The crocodile said: "Yes, it was like that. And after a while it begins to hurt." Boaji said: "I cannot judge that yet. The hunter had better lead you back into the bush. I will come with you." The hunter picked up the thong and led the crocodile into the bush. Finally they came to the place where he and the crocodile had met. The hunter said: "It was here." Boaji said: "Was it here?" The crocodile said: "Yes, it was here. From here on the hunter dragged me behind him to the river." Boaji said: "And you were not satisfied." The crocodile said: "No, I was not satisfied." Boaji said: "Good. You punished the hunter for his bad treatment of you by grabbing his foot and dragging him to the sandbank. So now the matter is in order. In order

to avoid further quarrels of this kind the hunter must un-
bind the thong and leave you here in the bush. That is
my decision."

Boaji and the hunter went off. The crocodile stayed
in the bush. The crocodile could not find the way back
to the river. The crocodile hungered and thirsted. The
hunter thanked Boaji.

There comes a time for every man when he is treated
as he has treated others.

Haussa Legend

THE OLD WOMAN

Into the land of Matasu there came a man who could not see, a Makapho, a blind man. The Makapho passed through the gate into the city and there he met an old woman who had her house near the city wall. The Makapho was going along the street when the old woman saw him, and when the old woman saw that he was blind she said to herself: "That is good."

The old woman went to the Makapho and said: "You are blind. Everyone helps the blind and Allah will be good to me if I take care of you. Come to my house and live with me." The Makapho said: "Very well, I'll live with you. The only thing I possess is this basket." And the old one answered: "Come along, now, I'll show you your room." The old woman brought him home.

The blind man then said to the old woman: "I'll go out immediately and see if I can earn something. Meanwhile, I've brought a hen with me in that basket there. Will you take it out of the basket, look after it and see if it lays any eggs?" The old woman answered: "I'll do that very thing. Allah will be good to me if I take care of you and your hen." The old woman took the hen. As soon as the blind man had gone she slaughtered it, cooked it and prepared a good meal which she devoured.

When the blind man, who had spent all day in the
market, came home that night to the old woman he asked:
"How is my hen?" "The hen! The hen!" the old woman
said. "That miserable hen. A jackal caught your hen, my
Makapho, and ate it up." The blind man said: "Allah will
help me with my hen."

The next day the blind man rose early and said to the
old woman: "I'll go out at once and see if I can earn
something." And the old woman answered: "Do that,
my Makapho; everyone gives gladly to the blind! Go,
then, and people will give you plenty." The blind man
went. He went through the town. He met a rich man.
The rich man had just told his servants to bring him his
goat to look at. The rich man looked at his goat. The
rich man saw the blind man and gave him the goat, saying: "Take the goat. Allah will be good to me for my
kindness." Makapho took the goat and went home.

When he came into the house with the goat he said to
the old woman: "Can you take my goat and look after
it for me?" And the old woman answered: "I'll do that
very thing. Allah will be good to me if I look after you
and your goat." The old woman took the goat and as
soon as the blind man had gone out again she took it to
the butcher. The butcher slaughtered it and sold the
meat.

At night when the Makapho returned to the old woman he asked: "How is my goat?" The old woman answered: "The goat! The goat! The wretched goat!

Kurra, the hyena caught it and tore it to pieces." The
blind man said: "Allah will help me with my goat."

The next day the blind man rose early and told the old
woman: "I'll go out at once and see what I can earn."
The old woman answered: "Do that, my Makapho.
Everyone gives gladly to the blind. Go then. The people
will give you richly." The blind man went. He went
through the city and encountered a Madugu, a leader
of a caravan. The Madugu had come to the city with
many heavily laden donkeys, had sold everything and
was now rich. The Madugu counted up what he had
earned. Then he saw the blind man. The Madugu took
a donkey, gave it to the blind man and said: "Take this
donkey. Allah will reward me for it." Makapho took
the donkey and went home with it.

Makapho came home with the donkey and asked the
old woman: "Can you take my donkey and look after
it for me?" And the old woman answered: "I'll do that
very thing. Allah will reward me if I take care of you
and your donkey." The old woman took the donkey.
The blind man went out again. As soon as he was gone
the old woman took the donkey and brought it to the
Ssongo (where the dealers are). At the Ssongo she
asked: "Is there no one here who will buy a good donkey?" The people came and looked at the donkey. A
man bought the donkey, the old woman took the money
and went home.

When the Makapho returned that evening he asked
the old woman: "How is my donkey?" The old woman

said: "Oh, the donkey! The unfortunate donkey! I
gave him something to eat. I must have given him too
much for he became very strong, broke the rope that
held him and ran away." Makapho said: "Then I'll go
and look for him." The old woman said: "My poor
Makapho, remember that you are blind. I have run around
and looked for him. And I can see. But I did not find the
donkey. So how do you expect to find him." The blind
man said: "You are right. But Allah will help me to get
my donkey back."

The next day the blind man rose early and told the
old woman: "I will go out at once and see what I can
earn." And the old woman answered: "Do that, my
Makapho. Everyone gives gladly to the blind. Go then,
the people will give you freely." The blind man went.
He went through the town. The blind man met the Galadima (head of the city). The Galadima's first wife had
just given birth to a child. It was the Galadima's first
son. Everyone came and congratulated him. The Galadima received all the wealthy people. Then he saw the
blind man and said: "Bring me a horse." They brought
him a horse. The Galadima said: "Give the horse to the
blind man. I make him a present of it and Allah will reward me for it." Makapho took the horse. Makapho
took the horse home.

Makapho came home with the horse and said to the
old woman: "Can you take my horse? Can you tie my
horse up and look after it for me?" The old woman said:
"I'll do that very thing. Allah will reward me if I take

care of you and your horse." The old woman took the horse. The blind man went out again. When he was gone the old woman took the horse and brought it to Serki Kassua (the market chief). The old woman said to Serki Kassua: "Here is a good horse. A stranger gave it to me to sell." Serki Kassua looked at the horse. The old woman said: "You can see that it is a young horse." Serki Kassua looked at the horse. The old woman said: "You can see it is a large horse." Serki Kassua looked at the horse. The old woman said: "You can see that it is a strong horse." Serki Kassua looked at the horse. Serki Kassua bought the horse. The old woman called two men to carry the money home for her.

In the evening when the blind man came home to the old woman he asked her: "How is my horse?" The old woman said: "Keep quiet. Do not talk so loudly or someone will hear you." The blind man said: "I am only asking how my horse is. What's the matter with my horse?" The old woman said: "Keep quiet. I say be quiet so that no one may hear you. One of the great men of the city came by. The great man saw the horse. The great man took the horse for himself." The blind man said: "I'll inquire for the horse at once, the horse that the Galadima gave me." The old woman said: "My poor Makapho. Remember that you are blind. Remember that the man is a great man in the city. If you go to him he will only do us harm." The blind man said: "You are right. I am blind. But Allah will help me with my horse."

The next morning the blind man rose early. Makapho

the blind man said to the old woman: "I'll go out at once
and see if I can earn something." The old woman said:
"Do that, my Makapho. Everyone gives gladly to the
blind. Go, then, the people will give you plenty." The
blind man went. He went across the market. He went
further. And so he met riders and soldiers. He met
Jerima, the crown prince, in the midst of the Lafidi, the
armored knights. Jerima was returning from the war.
Jerima had laid waste a city and had captured camels and
horses. Jerima saw the blind man. He waved to his followers and said: "Bring me that large camel that we
captured." The camel was brought before him. Jerima
gave the camel to Makapho and said: "Take the camel.
Allah will reward me for it." Makapho took the camel.
Makapho took the camel home.

Makapho came home with the camel and said to the
old woman: "I've just received a very fine camel as a
present from the Jerima. Can you take good care of the
camel so that it cannot run away or cannot be stolen?"
The old woman said: "I can do that very thing. You'll
find your camel here when you come home again. Allah
is witness to what I say." Makapho gave the old woman
the camel. The old woman tied it up by the side of the
house. Makapho went away again.

When the blind man had gone the old woman unbound
the camel and took it to the stream to drink. The old
woman gave the camel poison so that it might die. But
the camel did not die. The old woman gave the camel
still more poison. But the camel did not want to die. The

old woman took a lot of poison and shoved it down the camel's throat. The camel did not die, but it lay down and began to bellow. Then the old woman called to some men who were passing and said: "Come, come, the blind man's camel is dying. Come here and kill it so that it may die quickly." The men came close. They saw that the camel was very sick. The men killed the camel with their lances. Then they tied the legs of the camel with ropes and dragged it into the town. They came to the old woman's house. The old woman said: "Leave the camel here in front of the door. Allah will reward you for the service which you have rendered the blind man."

In the evening Makapho came home to the old woman. The blind man stumbled against the legs of the dead camel. The blind man said: "Kai! (Hey there) old woman. Do you put firewood across your threshold when a blind man lives in your house? Shall the blind man fall and break his legs?" The old woman said: "Have you ever seen firewood with legs and a head?" The blind man asked: "How is that?" The old woman answered: "Feel it, take hold of it and you'll find out. The firewood is your camel. The camel is dead. They gave you a wounded camel with a lance wound in its side." The blind man touched the camel, nodded his head and said: "Allah will help me with my camel."

The next morning the blind man rose early. He said to the old woman: "I'll go out at once and see if I can earn something." The old woman said: "Do that, my Makapho. Everyone gives gladly to the blind. Go, then,

the people will give you plenty." The blind man went.
The blind man went through the city. The blind man
came to the house of the king.

It was the day of the great Salla (New Year) cele-
bration. The noble and the wealthy went in to see the
king and greeted him. The king gave food to each. To
one he gave a horse, to another a garment. Makapho sat
at the entrance to the hall. The king saw Makapho and
said to his people: "Call me the blind one here." His
servants brought the blind man. The king said: "Today
is the great Salla. I will give the blind man a great present.
Bring me a maiden. Bring me one of my most beautiful
maidens." The maiden was brought. The king looked at
her and said: "Yes, that's what I want. I'll give this lovely
maiden to the blind man. My blind man, take this maiden
and marry her. I give her to you. Alla will reward me for
it." Makapho took the maiden. He took her home with
him.

Makapho brought the maiden into the house and said
to the old woman: "Look at the maiden, a lovely maiden.
Today is the great Salla. The king gave her to me to
marry. Will you take care of her?" The old woman said:
"I'll take care of the maiden, and in a way you won't easily
imagine. You'll see when you return. Allah is witness
to what I say." The blind man said: "You mean to say
that no wild beast will take her, that no man will steal
her and that she will not get lost?" And the old woman
answered: "No beast shall take her, if you do not regard me as a beast. No man shall take her away if I do

not give her away myself. And I must be worse than the devil if she gets lost!"

The blind man said: "No one will believe that you are worse and stronger than the devil. Here, take the maiden." And the blind man went out again.

When the blind man had gone the old woman said to the maiden: "You are a very lovely maiden. I have promised Makapho to take care of you. I will take care of you. Do you want to marry today?" The maiden said: "The king said I should marry today. I want to marry today." The old woman said: "Then wait here for a little while." The old woman locked up the maiden in her house. The old woman ran to a young man who had a great deal of money and always wore beautiful clothes and slept at night with beautiful maidens. The young man's house was scented because so much Muardi, a perfumed water, had been sprinkled there, and noisy because other young people came together there. The old woman ran to this young man.

The old woman said to the young man: "Have you still something left of that which you inherited from your father?" The young man said: "What girl do you want to bring me? I know all the Karua (whores) in the town. I do not want any more Karua." The old woman said: "I have another maiden: she is no Karua. She is a maiden lovelier than any in the town." The young man asked: "Which maiden is she?" The old woman said: "This maiden has never lived with a man." The young man said: "I still have a good part of that which my father

left me." The old woman said: "The king himself gave
the maiden away because she was the loveliest of all and
because today is the great Salla. But the man to whom
he gave her shall not have her." The young man said:
"I'll give you 500,000 cowrie shells." The old woman
said: "This maiden will be the greatest delicacy for him
who has her. He will be able to enjoy her again and
again, day after day. He will never be satiated with her."
The young man said: "I'll go to my friends and borrow
the money. I can give you 200,000 cowrie now." The
old woman asked: "Will you bring the money later?"
The young man said: "I'll send people to you with the
money." The old woman said: "That will be fine."

The old woman went home. The old woman went into
her house and seated herself on the lovely maiden's bed.
The old woman said to the maiden: "Have you seen the
man you are to marry?" And the maiden answered:
"I've seen the Makapho." The old woman said: "I know
a young man who is strong and handsome, his hands are
white and his face is like an Arab lady's. The young man
is rich. His house perfumes a whole quarter of the town,
so much Muardi has he sprinkled there. His people eat
good meat every day and he gives women to his slaves.
All the women of the city have run after this young man
and the Karua wanted to give him vast sums if he would
let them sleep with him. But the young man has had
enough of that. The young man asked me if I did not
know of a beautiful young maiden for him."

The maiden asked: "Does the young man live in this

town?" The old woman answered: "Yes, the young man lives in this town. . . . But tell me, my beauty, do you know that your Makapho has nothing and goes out daily to beg his bread?" The maiden answered: "Yes, I know that." The old woman said:" Then you know that you must lead him. You know that you must wear old clothes because he is poor." The young maiden said: "Yes, I know." The old woman said: "You have seen the Makapho. You know that his clothes are old and torn. You have seen that he has scars on his legs and feet and shoulders because a blind man in the street falls over stones and bumps into trees and walls." The young maiden said: "Yes, I know." The old woman said: "If you ever have a lovely dress, if you decorate your hair he will not see it. If you give yourself the trouble to paint your toes he will not see them. If you paint your eyes with kolli he won't see it. If you paint your brow with katambiri he won't see it. If you laugh he will not see it, nor will he hear it either for he will be worrying about whether people will give him food. If you cry he will beat you and say: 'How dare you cry when you can see? I am poor and blind and I do not cry.' And when you bear children he will go off and say: 'How will I be able to beg more food for them?' And he'll put your children on the street to beg for themselves. Do you know that?"

The young maiden threw herself on the ground and wept and cried: "My old mother, I beg you, I beg you! Bring me quickly to the young man." The old woman said: "Wait a while." The old woman went out. She brought katambiri and with it she adorned the lovely maiden's brow. She brought kolli with which she circled the lovely maiden's eyes. She brought a dress which she put on the lovely maiden's body and she brought a shawl with which she decorated the lovely maiden's head.

The young man ran around the town. He begged his friends: "Lend me a few thousand cowrie, I am getting a new girl for us." Some lent him 2000 cowrie, others lent him 5000 cowrie and still others lent him 10,000 cowrie. The young man put all the money in a pile. And to it he added the rest of the money which he had inherited from his father. But there was still not enough money there. The young man called a few slaves. He sold a slave. Then he sent all the money to the old woman. He also sent the old woman four dresses and two chains of pearls. The old woman took the money. The old woman hid the money. The old woman took a dress and a string of pearls and gave them to the young maiden. The old woman said: "These are presents for you from the young man. Put them on. Now you look lovely. Come now, we'll hurry to the young man before Makapho comes." The old woman brought the lovely young maiden to the handsome young man. The handsome young man took the lovely young maiden. The handsome young man said to his slaves: "Throw the old woman out!" The old woman said: "One of these days you'll call me back again." The old woman went home.

That evening Makapho came home to the old woman. Makapho had been given a dress and he brought food with him. Makapho went into his room. Makapho said: "Maiden, where are you." Makapho said: "My maiden, you are ashamed. But I do not demand that you speak. I will find you even though I am blind." Makapho went to the bed. Makapho explored the bed with his hands. Makapho said: "My maiden, you are not on the bed. My maiden, you are ashamed. You are still a maiden. But I will find you, even though I am blind." Makapho scated himself on the bed and said: "My maiden, I am blind. My maiden, I am poor. But Allah blesses the blind if they are not evil. I am blind but I have never done an evil thing. I am blind but I have never deceived. I am blind but I have never been a Monafiki, a malicious gossip with a friendly front. I have never been bad. And for that reason Allah has always taken care of me. You will marry me but you will never have to go on the street for the whores to see and make friends with. You are becoming my wife on the day of the great Salla and therefore Allah will take care of us both. Maiden mine, be not ashamed. Maiden mine, come to me!"

Makapho said: "Maiden mine, where are you? Maiden mine, I am blind; it is not as it is when other people marry. Maiden mine, come to me."

Makapho said: "Maiden mine, you will that I find you. Maiden, I come." The blind man rose. The blind man went along the wall. He felt the wall and went to the other side of the room and felt the wall there. He felt along all the walls and did not find the maiden. Makapho sat down on the bed and said: "My maiden has gone out."

Makapho rose and went out to the court where other people lived. Makapho questioned them, saying: "I came here this morning with a maiden whom the king had given me. I brought the maiden here and went away to find a wedding dress for her. I returned with the wedding dress, but now I cannot find my maiden. Can you tell me where my maiden is?" Some of the people said: "I do not know." Others said: "The maiden must have gone away." Still others said: "Someone must have taken her away." Some said: "Someone must have spoken with the maiden." And others said: "It must be a deal." An old man said: "A blind man is easy to deceive." A small boy said: "They arrayed the maiden beautifully. It was a very lovely maiden." Makapho said: "Can one of you give me a very stout stick?" The old man gave him a stick and said: "Here, take this, but see to it that you do not get into trouble with the Alkali, the judge. Perhaps the wood of the stick will be harder than the bones of an old woman." The blind man said: "It is well."

The blind man took the stick and said: "Now comes the fight." The old man said: "My Makapho, remember the judge." Makapho said: "This is no concern of the Alkali." Makapho went to the old woman. He entered the old woman's house. The old woman said: "You have been away for a long time, my Makapho." The blind man said: "Where is my maiden? Where is my lovely maiden?" The old woman said: "That maiden! That maiden! That was no maiden. That was a whore." The blind man closed the door behind him and said: "Where is my maiden? Where is my lovely maiden?" The old woman shrieked: "The wicked maiden, the maiden was evil: She had a Facka, a paramour. The Facka came here and the maiden wanted to sleep with him in your room." The blind man went across to the old woman and said: "Where is my maiden? Where is my lovely maiden?" The old woman yelled: "That evil maiden! How could I hold such a wicked creature? Her Facka came. Her Facka beat me. Then they both went away." The blind man raised his stick and said: "My maiden, where is my lovely maiden?" The old woman threw herself on the ground and cried: "That evil maiden! She cursed me! She stole the last bit of money I had. I wasn't able to hold her." The blind man made as if to strike the old woman and she, in her fear, befouled the floor.

But the blind man did not strike. The blind man said: "It is better that I do not touch you now. You said: 'No animal shall take that maiden, if you do not look on me as a beast!' You said: 'No man shall take that maiden away if I do not give her to him!' You said: 'I must be worse than the devil if that maiden gets lost.' You are worse than the devil. But Allah will see if you can accomplish more than the devil can. With the theft of a chicken the evil of old age begins and with the death of many men it ends so long as Allah takes no steps to block its progress. Woe to you. And now I must see if Allah has chosen me to block your path." The blind man went out.

Makapho locked the door behind him. The old woman in the house began to scream. The blind man went away.

The blind man went to the king. The blind man said to
the king: "My king, lend me ten strong men." The king
said: "What do you want the ten strong men for? Do you
want to put a new roof on your house?" The blind man
said: "No, I wish to put no new roof upon my house. It
is not my affair. It is an affair of Allah's. Allah has de-
livered an old woman into my hands, an old woman worse
than the devil." The king said: "Then take the ten strong
men." The blind man left with the ten strong men. The
blind man went to the chief of the slaughterers' guild,
Serki Faua. The blind man said: "Give me ten kiri, ten
leather thongs with which the bulls are bound so that they
cannot defend themselves against the slaughterer." The
chief of the slaughterers' said: "What do you need ten
kiri for? Do you want to build a trap for lions?" The
blind man said: "No, I wish to build no trap for lions. It
is not my affair. It is an affair of Allah's. Allah has de-
livered an old woman into my hands, an old woman worse
than the devil. The king has lent me ten strong men."
The chief of the slaughterers' said: "Then take the ten
kiri."

The blind man went with the ten strong men and the
ten leather thongs to the house of the old woman. The
blind man unlocked the door. The blind man said to the
ten strong men: "Tie these thongs around the old
woman's body, around her head, around her arms and
around her legs. Beat her and kick her. Pull her back and
forth. Strangle her and stick her. Punch her and squeeze
her." The ten strong men bound the thongs around the

old woman's limbs and her head, around her neck and her body, and beat the old woman and kicked her. They pulled the old woman here and there. They throttled and poked her. They squeezed and punched her. The old woman screamed and the old woman yelled. The old woman puked blood. The old woman befouled the floor. The blind man said: "Now we will see whether with all this stink, the evil has come out of her, too. It is Allah's will that she be paid in her own coin."

The ten strong men let the old woman go. The ten strong men went away with the leather thongs. But the blind man lighted a fire in the old woman's house. He threw pepper on it. Then he went out and locked the door. The fire smoked. Thick smoke filled the room. In her fear the old woman ran from one side of the room to the other. The smoke filled the whole house. At first the old woman screamed, but then the smoke filled her throat. The old woman fell to the floor. Thereupon the blind man opened the door. He said: "It is not Allah's will that you die." The smoke went out of the house. The old woman stood up again.

The blind man called a barber and had him shave off the old woman's hair. The blind man did not let the barber use any water for it. Then the blind man took a heavy iron ring, laid it on the old woman's head and said: "That is your useka.* And now I will give you a load." The

* Useka is the soft ring cushion, of leather or cloth filled with silk, which the Haussa lay on their heads when they have to carry a heavy load.

blind man gave the old woman a heavy stone which she
had to carry on her head with the iron ring as a cushion.
The blind man said: "Now go into the country round
about and trade." The old woman had to go. The blind
man drove her before him. For seven months the old
woman had to carry the stone on her head. Then the
blind man said to her: "Now throw the stone and the
iron ring away. You followed the path of theft from the
stolen chicken to the stolen girl. Then Allah threw this
stone in your path. My quarrel with you is at an end.
I will not do anything more to you. I am going my way.
And go you yours."

Makapho went. The old woman threw the stone and
the iron ring away. The old woman said: "This blind
man is very stupid. But I'll go home quickly and see if my
money is still there." The old woman went back to the
town. The old woman went to the market and sold spice.
She had spice for sale at the market. Iblis the devil appeared in the market. The devil came to the old woman
and said: "That was a bad affair you had with Makapho."
The old woman said: "Kai! Don't laugh at me! You may
be strong but I can outdo you." The devil said: "How is
that? Don't you, the old woman from Matusu, recognize
me?" The old woman said: "Why shouldn't I know
you? You are the devil. But even if you are the devil,
were your head, your limbs and your body ever tied with
ten leather thongs? Have ten strong men ever punched
and kicked and squeezed and pinched and beaten you?
Were you ever shut in a room with fire and pepper smoke

for so long that the smoke filled your throat and you fell unconscious? Have you ever had your skull dry shaved and an iron ring laid on it, and have you ever had to carry a heavy stone for seven months on that iron ring? Kai! Devil, could you stand that?"

The devil said: "What are your other big achievements?" The old woman said: "What are my other big achievements? I do not recall them all. But this much I remember. I have estranged more than eleven thousand people who were married and have made them hate each other. I have so antagonized two thousand people, who were courting each other, that they never met again, never married and had children." The devil said: "That's a pretty good record, my old woman. That's really fine. But that is no reason for you to say that you outdo me. I'll give you an example here on the market of something you won't be able to copy. For I am Iblis, the devil." The old woman said: "You are the devil and competent enough, that I know. And you will probably do a pretty big thing, that I know. Whether I can imitate it or outdo it, I cannot say — for you were never tied with ten leather thongs and never sat in pepper smoke. You never had to carry a rocky weight on an iron ring on a shorn head for months at a time. So I'll wait before I say anything till you've done what you are going to do." The old woman packed up her market basket and went home.

The devil wandered around the market. He sat down and listened to what the girls who sold kola nuts were saying. He sat down and listened to what the clothes

makers were saying. Iblis went to where the linen dealers
sat, crouched nearby and listened to what was said. Iblis
listened to what the people of the town said, and he heard
what the heathen Magussaua, who had come with their
women to the market to sell sheep and wood and Dauwa,
related. Iblis listened to all of them. Some quarrelled mali-
ciously. Some spoke well of each other and some related
evil of each other. But Iblis was on the watch only for the
evil words they spoke. Iblis went to a group of people.
Iblis said: "You bought that from that man over there. I
heard him say how he had cheated you." Iblis went to
another group and said: "This man cheated that man and
you ought to do something about it." Iblis went to others
and said: "Those people say that one of you cheated
them. But they only say it because one of them misused
one of your women when she brought him food the other
evening." Iblis went to others and said: "You must help
these people against those, for those are evil and say evil
for they have done evil things." Iblis went to a well respected man whose caravans plied here and there all over
the country. He said to this man: "People say that you
are a malicious gossip who starts quarrels between people
because you don't get enough money from them." The
man was really a monafiki, a mischief, and outside of that
he was used to taking the last bit of money that people
had so that they had to bond themselves and were never
able to earn their freedom again.

But when the monafiki heard the devil say what had
been said he drew his sword. The monafiki ran to the

people who had gossiped about him and cried: "Who called me a monafiki?" There was a man there who had long been in bondage to the monafiki and who now had no more to lose. This man cried: "You are a monafiki! It is true! You are a monafiki! I'll repeat it before everyone. Everyone shall hear it!" The monafiki struck at the man with his sword. The rich monafiki struck the poor man. Whereupon some of the people cried: "First this man took our money. Now he takes our lives!"

A few people struck at the rich monafiki. The monafiki's slaves ran to help him. The rich monafiki fell to the earth. A few shouted with pleasure. Others shouted in protest. Some cried: "This man cheated that one." Others shouted: "And that one misused this one's woman!" All began to strike out. Each one grabbed whatever weapon lay to hand. Finally twelve hundred people were killed. Then the Dogari, the king's bodyguard, came and drove all the people away from the market.

The devil went to the old woman and said: "Come with me and I will show you what I can do in a single day." The old woman went with the devil. The devil led the old woman to the market. On the ground there lay baskets and clothes, kola nuts and bean cakes, shoes and mealcakes, roast meat and thread. The dead lay here and there. And everywhere the Dogari were patroling back and forth among the chaos of goods and bodies on the blood-stained ground. The devil said to the old woman: "See now, I did all that in a single day."

The old woman looked around the market place. The old woman said: "That is no more than twelve hundred dead and a wrecked market." The devil said: "Yes, it is twelve hundred dead and a wrecked market." The devil said: "And I did all of it in a single day." The old woman turned away in contempt and said: "Is that all? Do you think you can do more than I can with that? Devil, go home. Go home. Come again tomorrow evening and then I'll show you what the old woman can do."

The next morning the old woman went out and bought a hundred first-rate kola nuts; she bought a jar full of perfumed water; she bought a handful of truare-djubuda (civet excretion). Of all this the old woman took fifty of the kola nuts and the truare-djubuda and set out for the house of the king. The Serki, as the king was called, had married a young wife not long before. The young maiden whom he had married was particularly lovely, so lovely that all the people of the town spoke of her, and the king liked her so well that he preferred her to his other wives and set her beside his first wife.

The old woman came to the king's young wife. The old woman looked at the young wife of the king. The old woman said: "Now that I have seen you I understand his words, the words of Susso, words which at first seemed crazy to me." The young woman said: "What is the matter with me?" The old woman said: "You are very lovely. You are lovelier than all other women. And now that I have seen you I understand the words which at first seemed crazy to me." The young wife of the king said:

"Kai, old woman! You cannot say such things here. You
are in the court of the king. Come, I'll give you a shawl.
Now tell me quickly a bit of gossip from the town and
then go." The old woman looked at the lovely wife of
the king. The old woman said: "Yes, he said too: 'You
will go into the house of an old man, the king.' He said:
'There you will see the young wife of the king, lovelier
than all other women.' Now that I have seen you I understand the words that seemed crazy to me before." The
king's young wife said: "Quickly now, tell me something
new."

The old woman put down the fifty kola nuts and the
truare-djubuda and said: "What else can he send you
but a trifle! You have everything. And should he give
you a golden ring, the king would see it." The young wife
asked: "Who sends that here? How dare anyone send
anything here in my house?" The old woman said:
"Only one man can do that. No other young man in the
town would dare to send a kola nut to this house of the
king, into the house where the old king has shut you up!"
The young wife of the king said: "Who sends you?"
The old woman answered: "It can be only he who rides
at the front in war. It can be only he whose coming the
enemy fears more than that of a thousand other riders."
The young wife of the king said: "Who sends you
here?" The old woman said: "He who sends me is the
son of the Jerima."

The young wife of the king said: "Does not the son
of the Jerima fear to send this to the favorite wife of the

king?" The old woman said: "If a hundred lions charge him the son of the Jerima will have no fear. If a hundred elephants charge him the son of the Jerima will have no fear. Why should he then be afraid of an old man?" The young wife of the king said: "What thinks the son of the Jerima?" The old woman said: "The son of the Jerima thinks no more of prayer. The son of the Jerima thinks no more of his father and mother. The son of the Jerima thinks only of you!"

The young wife of the king took the kola nuts. The young wife of the king took the truare-djubuda. The young wife of the king said: "Whenever my white teeth bite into these kola nuts, then I will think of the son of the Jerima. When the perfume of the truare-djubuda permeates my garments I will think of the son of the Jerima." The old woman answered: "Think of him when you hear that he is going to the wars again. Think of him when you hear that he has been killed in battle." The young wife of the king said: "Is the son of the Jerima going to the wars again soon?" The old woman said: "The son of the Jerima does not wish to live any longer. He thinks only of you. He is going to the wars again to-morrow. And he will not return." The young wife of the king said: "He will not return?" The old woman said: "No, the son of the Jerima will not return to this city, the city in which you live shut up in the walls of the king's house. The son of the Jerima wishes to die."

The young wife of the king said: "He will let himself be slain in battle!" The young wife of the king wept.

The young wife of the king said: "Tell me, old woman, how will it be possible for me to see the son of the Jerima today?" The old woman said: "That is a difficult thing. The son of the Jerima told me: 'How is it possible for me to see the young wife of the king again before I go to the wars?' That is a difficult thing." The young wife of the king said: "You, old woman! The son of the Jerima dare not let himself be killed in battle! You, old woman, I must see the son of the Jerima today, today! Listen, old woman, when I want the king to do something, he does it. Tell me now how it will be possible for me to see the son of the Jerima today."

The old woman said: "O young and beautiful wife of the king, go you to the king and say: 'I hear that my mother is ill. Permit me to go to her. Before evening falls I will return.' And when the king has given you permission, then come quickly to me in the small house by the city wall." The young wife of the king said: "Yes, that is what I will do. I'll go to the king at once. And then I will come to you in the small house by the city wall." The old woman said: "Come to me. And then I will go to the son of the Jerima and tell him that you are in my house."

The young wife of the king gave the old woman a headshawl and a dress. The old woman went. The young wife of the king took the kola nuts. She took a shawl and laid four of the nuts in the shawl. The young wife of the king said: "The son of the Jerima is young and handsome." The young woman took four more nuts, laid

them in the shawl and said: "The king is old." The young
woman took four other nuts, laid them in the shawl and
said: "The son of the Jerima said that I was the most
beautiful woman in all the city." The young wife took
four more nuts, laid them in the shawl and said: "The
son of the Jerima shall not go to war." The young wife
took four more kola nuts, laid them in the shawl and said:
"I will beg the young son of the Jerima not to go to war."
The young wife of the king took the remaining nuts,
threw them into the shawl and said: "Now I am going
to the son of the Jerima. Now I'll throw myself to the
ground before the son of the Jerima. Now I'll beg him
and beg him and beg him. Now I'll go and make myself
beautiful, and now I know at last for whom I am doing
it!"

The young wife of the king threw off her clothes. The
young wife of the king put on lovely garments and then
put on old clothes over them. With her lovely garments
hidden by the old clothes she left the house. She went into
a house of the king. She told a slave: "Go tell the king
that I must see him!" The slave said: "This is not the
time for that. The king is giving audience." The young
woman said: "Kai, slave, go — or I'll go myself and ask
the king to have you thrashed. Go to the king and tell
him: 'Your young wife will speak with you. Your young
wife fears a death.' Go!" The slave went to the king's
audience chamber. All the influential people sat there
around him. The slave threw himself to the ground before
the king. The king said: "What is the matter?" The

slave said: "Your young wife will speak with you. Your young wife fears a death." The king stood up. The king went out. The Tschiroma, a princely chamberlain, said to the Galadima of the city: "The king is getting old. Any woman can do what she wants with him." The Galadima said: "Yes, the king is getting old."

The king entered the house in which the young woman was waiting for him. The young woman threw herself to the ground before the king. The young wife wept and said: "Serki! Serki! Serki! King! King! King!" The king said: "You weep and wear old clothes! Haven't I given you enough new and beautiful garments?" The young wife wept and cried: "King! King! King!" The king bent over her and raised her to her feet. The king said: "What's the matter?" The young wife cried: "I fear a death! I fear a death! I fear a death!" The king said: "Why shall you die?" The young wife wept and said: "I won't be the first to die. But a person dies and then another person must die, too." The king asked: "Who, then?" The young wife wept and said: "Allow me to go to my mother. Let me go at once. I have just had news. I'll be back again this evening." The king said: "Has your mother been ill for long?" The young wife wept and said: "No, but may I go?" The king said: "Go." The young woman hurried away.

The young wife ran through the court. The young wife ran through the city. The young wife ran to the end of the city. The young wife ran to the small house by the city wall. The young woman entered the old woman's house. The old woman said: "You! But why do you come in poor old clothes?" The young wife said: "Never mind! Go quickly and call the son of the Jerima!" The old woman went. The old woman went through the city and said to herself: "The hunter in the bush has fired a stalk of grass on the steppe. Soon comes the wind. The wind will drive the fire through the bush, and the fire will destroy the homesteads and the granaries of the people."

The old woman ran through the city. The old woman ran into the Jerima's court. The Jerima had but one son. And the son of the Jerima was in his house. The slaves of the Jerima sat before him and sharpened his swords and daggers and lances. The old woman threw herself to the ground before the son of the Jerima. The old woman lay there. The son of the Jerima said: "What is wrong?" The old woman said: "The son of the Jerima fears not and robs the lion of its cub." The son of the Jerima said: "What is the matter?" The old woman said: "What two ears would like to hear need not necessarily be shared by eight." The son of the Jerima said to the slaves: "Get out!" The slaves got out.

The Jerima's slaves went out. The son of the Jerima said: "What's up?" The old woman took the fifty kola nuts out of her headshawl. The old woman set the jar of perfumed water before him. The old woman said: "That is sent by a young woman." The son of the Jerima said: "What are you trying to say?" The old woman said: "You shall not go to war. You shall not die. For if one person dies then another must die, too, for the one can-

A finely accoutred bowman in a Southwest Africa rock painting.

not live if the other does not return." The son of the Jerima stood up. The son of the Jerima said: "Who is the young woman? Isn't her man good enough for her?" The old woman said: "The young woman always looks over the wall when you go forth to war. The young woman cannot sleep when you are in battle. She suffers in the night when you are at the wars. The young woman looks over the wall when you return. Then she can live again by day. When you are at the wars the young woman gives presents to beggars and the blind, so that Allah may help you. And when you return from the wars the young woman gives presents to beggars and the blind, so that Allah may keep you in the city."

The son of the Jerima said: "Old woman, tell me who the young woman is!" The old woman said: "She is the most beautiful woman in the city. But she lies between the lion's paws. Only a brave one may see her and greet her." The son of the Jerima took his sword and raised it. The son of the Jerima said: "Old woman, tell me quickly who the young woman is." The old woman said: "It is the young wife of the king." The son of the Jerima said: "The young wife of the king!?" The son of the Jerima threw his sword away. The son of the Jerima said: "Where is the lovely young wife of the king?" The old woman said: "The lovely young wife of the king is in my house. The beautiful young woman is sitting on the edge of the bed." The son of the Jerima said: "Lead on! Show me the way!"

The old woman went. The son of the Jerima took a

man of his father's with him. The son of the Jerima and
the man followed the old woman. The old woman and
the man and the son of the Jerima went through the city.
They came to the city wall. The man withdrew. The old
woman opened the door of her house. The young wife
rose from the side of the bed. The son of the Jerima went
in the door. The young woman let the old clothes fall to
the ground. The young woman stood before the son of
the Jerima. She was very beautiful. And she wore lovely
garments. The old woman shut the door. The son of the
Jerima stayed there, in the house, with the lovely young
wife of the king.

The Jerima's man stood outside. The door of the old
woman's house was on the latch. The old woman ran
away. The old woman ran through the city. The old
woman ran to the royal quarters. The influential people
had greeted the king and the king had reached them the
morning dish. The king had retired to an inner chamber.
The prominent people were gone. The king was alone.
The old woman ran through the corridor. The old woman
ran into the chamber in which the king sat. The old
woman threw herself to the ground and cried: "O, King!
King! King!" The old woman wailed and cried: "Now
you'll kill me for it!" The king said: "Why should I
kill you?" The old woman cried: "You will kill me because others deceive you." The king said: "What is the
matter?" The old woman wept and said: "How can I
help it that the son of the Jerima does not respect you?"
The king said: "In what way does he not respect me?"

The old woman wept and said: "If only the son of the
Jerima would play around with other people's wives!
Couldn't the son of the Jerima leave at least this one lovely
young wife alone? Must the son of the Jerima devote
himself to just this one particular beautiful young wife
whom you love above all others and have placed at the
side of your first wife?" The king said: "Old woman, tell
me the truth. Tell me if you have seen the son of the
Jerima with my wife." The king said: "Old woman, tell
me the truth!" The old woman said: "They are in my
house!" The king shouted: "You lie!" The old woman
said: "Look at my white hair; I cannot lie. At this very
moment they are sitting on my bed in my house." The
king said: "I'll send a messenger to see." The king called
one of his men. The king said: "Go with the old woman
and see whether it is true that the son of the Jerima is
courting my wife in the old woman's house." The messenger took a dagger. The messenger went with the old
woman.

The old woman led the king's messenger to her small
house by the city wall. At some distance from the house
stood the Jerima's man. The king's messenger went to the
door of the old woman's house. He opened it. The king's
messenger saw the son of the Jerima. The king's messenger saw the lovely young wife of the king. But the
lovely young wife of the king and the son of the Jerima
did not see the king's messenger. For they had eyes only
for each other. The king's messenger drew his dagger.
The king's messenger stabbed the son of the Jerima in

the back. The blood spurted out and poured over the lovely young wife of the king. The lovely young wife screamed. The son of the Jerima said : "That's a rotten way to die!" The son of the Jerima was dead.

The old woman stood outside with the Jerima's man. The son of the Jerima said : "That's a rotten way to die." The Jerima's man heard it. The Jerima's man rushed into the house and struck down the king's messenger. Then the Jerima's man tripped over the clothes of the young wife of the king which were lying on the floor and fell to the ground. The old woman ran away. The old woman ran through the city. The old woman ran as fast as she could. The old woman said to herself : "Now the wind is driving the flames over the homesteads and granaries of the people. Nothing of this city shall remain." The old woman ran as fast as she could.

The old woman ran into the house of the Jerima. The old woman cried : "Jerima, why haven't you saddled your horse ?" The Jerima replied : "Why should I saddle my horse, old woman ?" The old woman said : "Will you then go to war on foot, like a common soldier ?" The Jerima said : "Who is making war ?" The old woman said : "When the king wanted to sack a foreign city you rode ahead and were the first. But now, now when the king has had your son killed you stay there lying on your mat." The Jerima leapt to his feet. The old woman said : "Was not this son your only son ?" The Jerima cried : "Saddle my horse! Saddle my horse!"

The old woman ran out. The old woman ran through

the streets. The old woman ran as fast as she could. The old woman said to herself : "Now the wind is driving the flames over the granaries and homesteads of the people. Nothing shall remain of this city." The old woman ran as fast as she could.

The old woman ran into the house of the king. The old woman yelled down the royal corridor : "O, King! King! King! Saddle your horse!" The king said : "What's wrong, then ?" The old woman said : "King you were. King you are no longer ! The Jerima has slain your messenger. The Jerima is to horse. The Jerima is riding through the city with his knights." The king called : "Dig a grave for a king !" The old woman ran away. The old woman said to herself : "Now I'll heap wood and dry grass on the flames." The old woman ran as fast as she could.

The old woman ran to where the beggars and thieves lived. The old woman called the beggars and thieves together. The old woman said : "When the great beasts have killed each other the worms feast on their bodies." The beggars and thieves said : "What's up ?" The old woman said : "Hear the drums beat. Hear the noise of the horsemen. The king and the Jerima have started a war. Everyone is in the streets." The beggars and thieves said : "Well, we aren't here to fight. Let the others fight. What are we to do ?" The old woman said : "All the men are in the streets. No one is watching the houses. Go here and there. Fire the houses. Steal clothes and pearls, steal silver and gold." The beggars and thieves said : "The old

woman is right. We'll do that." The old woman said:
"What sort of women can you afford? Think of the
women you can have today. All the men are in the streets.
Throw their wives and daughters to the ground. You'll
find them better than the Karua!" The beggars and the
thieves ran off.

The beggars and the thieves ran off. All the menfolk
ran with weapons through the streets. Drums thundered.
Knights put the spurs to their horses. The Jerima collected his followers and rode with them to the royal
quarters. The king collected his followers and rode with
them against the house of the Jerima. The hostile parties
met. The Jerima cried: "You have slain my only son."
The king cried: "Your son made love to my young and
beautiful wife!" The king and the Jerima raised their
swords and charged. The king and the Jerima struck
home. The king and the Jerima fell from their horses.
The king and the Jerima died.

The king's followers yelled. The Jerima's followers
yelled. Some charged here; some charged there. Some
struck here; some fought there. Some lunged with lances;
others struck with clubs. Some shot arrows; others threw
stones. The women fled into their houses and hid their
children. The maidens fled into the granaries and store
rooms and crouched there together. But the beggars and
thieves ran through the city. The beggars and thieves
fired here a granary, there a house. The women shrieked;
the children screamed. The beggars and thieves went
into the houses. Some stole. Others threw maidens to the

floor. The men in the streets ran away to save their possessions. The flames were everywhere. Children were killed by arrows. Women were crushed by the horses. Many people were burned alive.

Houses and granaries burned and were destroyed. Men and women and children died. The mat walls roared in the flames. The women screamed in the street. Whoever could grab something ran out of the city. Dead men lay in the streets. Pillars of fire twisted over the courtyards. The beggars and thieves carried away what they found. Whoever could run fled through the gate in the city wall out into the bush.

The old woman stood on the city wall above the gate. The old woman danced. The old woman sang. The old woman sang: "I haven't danced once since I was young. Since I was young I haven't once danced. But today I'll be king of the city and Kurra, the hyena, and Angulu, the buzzard, will prostrate themselves before me and cry: 'King! King! King!' They'll thank me for the feast that I brought them with this fire. They'll thank me for the bones which I will throw to them. Kai! Makapho! You had ten men bind me with ten leather thongs around my limbs, my head, my neck and my body. The ten strong men beat me and kicked me, squeezed me and punched me, pinched me and choked me. Kai! Makapho! You shut me in a room with pepper smoke and fire till my throat was filled with smoke and I fell down. Kai! Makapho! On my dry shaved skull you laid an iron ring as a cushion for a heavy stone that I had to carry for seven months long. Kai! Makapho! Look at the city in which you lost your chicken, your goat and donkey and horse and camel! Kai! Makapho! You taught me all that!"

The old woman danced on the city wall above the city gate. The town was burnt. The people either lay around as corpses or had run away. The old woman danced and sang: "Kai! Iblis! Now come and see what an old woman can do. Kai! Iblis! Haven't I outdone you?" The devil came.

The devil climbed to the top of the city wall. The devil looked down on the city. The devil saw the corpses and the burned houses. In the center of the city lay the dead king and the dead Jerima side by side. Not a person lived within the city. The hyenas crept up through the bush. The buzzards circled over the smoke in the still air.

The devil saw it all.

The devil said: "What, you a single old woman, have done all that in a single day? If you've just done that, what will you then do tomorrow?" The devil began to be afraid of the old woman. The devil sprang down. The devil disappeared into the earth. The old woman did not see him again.

The sun set.

PART THREE

THE SOUTHERN RHODESIANS

Ngona Horn Stories

THE MOON AND HIS WIVES

Maori (God) made the first man and called him Mwuetsi (moon). He put him on the bottom of a Dsivoa (lake) and gave him a ngona horn filled with ngona oil. Mwuetsi lived in Dsivoa.

Mwuetsi said to Maori: "I want to go on the earth." Maori said: "You will rue it." Mwuetsi said: "None the less, I want to go on the earth." Maori said: "Then go on the earth." Mwuetsi went out of Dsivoa and on to the earth.

The earth was cold and empty. There were no grasses, no bushes, no trees. There were no animals. Mwuetsi wept and said to Maori: "How shall I live here?" Maori said: "I warned you. You have started on the path at the end of which you shall die. I will, however, give you one of your kind." Maori gave Mwuetsi a maiden who was called Massassi, the morning star. Maori said: "Massassi shall be your wife for two years." Maori gave Massassi a fire-maker.

In the evening Mwuetsi went into a cave with Massassi. Massassi said: "Help me. We will make a fire. I will gather chimandra (kindling) and you can twirl the rusika (revolving part of the fire-maker)." Massassi

gathered kindling. Mwuetsi twirled the rusika. When the
fire was lighted Mwuetsi lay down on one side of it,
Massassi on the other. The fire burned between them.

Mwuetsi thought to himself : "Why has Maori given
me this maiden ? What shall I do with this maiden, Massassi ?" When it was night Mwuetsi took his ngona horn.
He moistened his index finger with a drop of ngona oil.
Mwuetsi said : "Ndini chaambuka mhiri ne mhiri." (I
am going to jump over the fire.)* Mwuetsi jumped over
the fire. Mwuetsi approached the maiden, Massassi.
Mwuetsi touched Massassi's body with the ointment on
his finger. Then Mwuetsi went back to his bed and slept.

When Mwuetsi wakened in the morning he looked
over to Massassi. Mwuetsi saw that Massassi's body was
swollen. When day broke Massassi began to bear. Massassi bore grasses. Massassi bore bushes. Massassi bore trees.
Massassi did not stop bearing till the earth was covered
with grasses, bushes and trees.

The trees grew. They grew till their tops reached the
sky. When the tops of the trees reached the sky it began
to rain.

Mwuetsi and Massassi lived in plenty. They had fruits
and grain. Mwuetsi built a house. Mwuetsi made an iron
shovel. Mwuetsi made a hoe and planted crops. Massassi
plaited fish traps and caught fish. Massassi fetched wood
and water. Massassi cooked. Thus Mwuetsi and Massassi
lived for two years.

---

* This sentence is many times repeated in a melodramatic, ceremonial
tone.

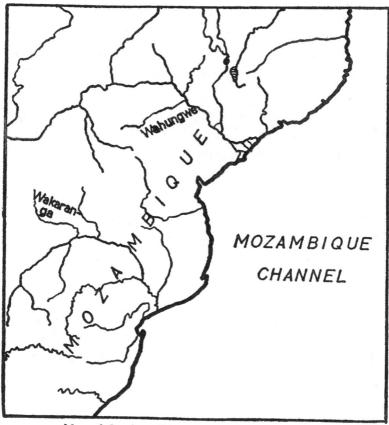

Map of Southern Rhodesian rock-picture section.

After two years Maori said to Massassi: "The time is up." Maori took Massassi from the earth and put her back in Dsivoa. Mwuetsi wailed. He wailed and wept and said to Maori: "What shall I do without Massassi. Who will fetch wood and water for me? Who will cook for me?" Eight days long Mwuetsi wept.

Eight days long Mwuetsi wept. Then Maori said: "I

have warned you that you are going to your death. But I
will give you another woman. I will give you Morongo,
the evening star. Morongo will stay with you for two
years. Then I shall take her back again." Maori gave
Mwuetsi Morongo.

Morongo came to Mwuetsi in the hut. In the evening
Mwuetsi wanted to lie down on his side of the fire. Mor-
ongo said: "Do not lie down over there. Lie with me."
Mwuetsi lay down beside Morongo. Mwuetsi took the
ngona horn, put some ointment on his index finger. But
Morongo said: "Don't be like that. I am not like Massassi.
Now smear your loins with ngona oil. Smear my loins
with ngona oil." Mwuetsi did as he was told. Morongo
said: "Now couple with me." Mwuetsi coupled with
Morongo. Mwuetsi went to sleep.

Towards morning Mwuetsi woke. As he looked over
to Morongo he saw that her body was swollen. As day
broke Morongo began to give birth. The first day Morongo gave birth to chickens, sheep, goats.

The second night Mwuetsi slept with Morongo again.
The next morning she bore eland and cattle.

The third night Mwuetsi slept with Morongo again.
The next morning Morongo bore first boys and then girls.
The boys who were born in the morning were grown up
by nightfall.

On the fourth night Mwuetsi wanted to sleep with
Morongo again. But there came a thunderstorm and
Maori spoke: "Let be. You are going quickly to your
death." Mwuetsi was afraid. The thunderstorm passed

over. When it had gone Morongo said to Mwuetsi: "Make a door and then use it to close the entrance to the hut. Then Maori will not be able to see what we are doing. Then you can sleep with me." Mwuetsi made a door. With it he closed the entrance to the hut. Then he slept with Morongo. Mwuetsi slept.

Towards morning Mwuetsi woke. Mwuetsi saw that Morongo's body was swollen. As day broke Morongo began to give birth. Morongo bore lions, leopards, snakes and scorpions. Maori saw it. Maori said to Mwuetsi: "I warned you."

On the fifth night Mwuetsi wanted to sleep with Morongo again. But Morongo said: "Look, your daughters are grown. Couple with your daughters." Mwuetsi looked at his daughters. He saw that they were beautiful and that they were grown up. So he slept with them. They bore children. The children which were born in the morning were full grown by night. And so Mwuetsi became the Mambo (king) of a great people.

But Morongo slept with the snake. Morongo no longer gave birth. She lived with the snake. One day Mwuetsi returned to Morongo and wanted to sleep with her. Morongo said: "Let be." Mwuetsi said: "But I want to." He lay with Morongo. Under Morongo's bed lay the snake. The snake bit Mwuetsi. Mwuetsi sickened.

After the snake had bitten Mwuetsi, Mwuetsi sickened. The next day it did not rain. The plants withered. The rivers and lakes dried. The animals died. The people began to die. Many people died. Mwuetsi's children

asked: "What can we do?" Mwuetsi's children said:
"We will consult the hakata (sacred dice)." The children
consulted the hakata. The hakata said: "Mwuetsi the
Mambo is sick and pining. Send Mwuetsi back to the
Dsivoa."

Thereupon Mwuetsi's children strangled Mwuetsi
and buried him. They buried Morongo with Mwuetsi.
Then they chose another man to be Mambo. Morongo,
too, had lived for two years in Mwuetsi's Zimbabwe.*

THE GIRL WITH A MOTHER'S HEART

There was a very poor man. Still, he had a horn full
of ngona oil. The man drank from the horn full of ngona
oil. The man said: "I will marry a maiden who has a
heart like a mother's. I want a wife who will never cause
me trouble. I want a wife who will not quarrel with me
when I spoil her clothes. I want a wife who will keep
everything clean and take good care of me."

The man set off. In another village he met a maiden
who pleased him. The man told the maiden: "I want to
marry you." The maiden said: "I am willing." The man
said: "It is not enough that you are willing. I will sleep
with you tonight to find out if you will suit me perma-
nently." That night the man slept with the maiden. During the night, as the maiden looked at him, she saw that

---

* Zimbabwe means, roughtly, "the royal court." The enormous prehistoric ruins near Fort Victoria are called "The Great Zimbabwe," other
stone ruins throughout Southern Rhodesia are called "Little Zimbabwe."

his body decayed and that worms crept over him. The maiden was terrified and fled from the hut. She ran to her mother and said: "Mother, the body of the man who will marry me decays and the worms are already creeping over it." The mother said: "That has occurred because you girls always run after the first stranger you see. In this case you will do well to stay at home with me."

Southern Rhodesian picture of mourners.

In the morning the maiden returned to the hut to see how it went with the stranger. The young man was already up and sat in the door of the hut. He said to the maiden: "Bring me water." The maiden brought him water. The young man washed himself and drank. The young man told the maiden: "You are not the maiden I will marry. You have not a mother's heart. But since you gave me a night, I will give you two arm rings." The young man gave the maiden two arm rings.

The young man came to another village. In the village lived a maiden somewhat older than the first one. Till now no young man had come to marry her. This maiden pleased the young man and he said: "I want to marry you. But first I want to try you out to see if you are the maiden I am looking for. Therefore you shall spend the night with me." The young man slept with the maiden. As the maiden woke up in the night she saw that the young man's body was rotting and that worms were creeping over it. When she saw this she cried: "The young man I love is dying." The maiden ran and fetched her kaembe (a calabash which is shaken like a rattle in accompaniment to song or dance). The maiden sat by the young man's body and sang and rattled the kaembe. The maiden sang all night. The maiden sang all day.

The following evening her parents came and said: "Why do you stay in this house? Why do you not come back to us?" The maiden said: "I cannot leave the man who loved me." The father said: "I will tell the chief of the village." The father went to the chief and said: "The stranger who came to our village has died." The chief said: "We will bury the stranger." The grave was dug. The body of the stranger was put in the grave and buried.

The people wanted to go home, but the maiden said: "I will stay here with my kaembe and sing by the grave of him who loved me." The maiden's mother said: "I stay where my daughter stays." The maiden's father said: "I cannot desert my family. I stay here." The uncle

Southern Rhodesian picture of man and weapons.

said: "I stand by my family." Other people said: "We cannot leave this family alone. We stay here, too." The chief said: "I must stay where the people of my village are. I remain here."

The young man in the grave heard everything that was said. He said to himself: "Now I can climb out of the grave. These are people among whom a maiden with a mother's heart can feel at home. I have found a maiden with a mother's heart." The young man rose out of the grave. The young man presented the maiden's father with a hoe. The young man said : "I thank you. I will marry your daughter." The young man gave the chief and every person in the village a hoe and thanked them. The chief of the village said : "I cannot allow that a man who dies, is buried and then rises from the grave remain my inferior." The young man married the maiden and became chief of the village.

THE HUNTER

A man went hunting with his friends. The others had luck and brought home plenty of game. But he had no luck at all and came home empty-handed. The man went hunting the next day and many days thereafter. But he was never successful. He never brought a buck home with him.

The man said : "What shall I do ? I had better get myself a muschonga." The man found a nganga (witch doctor). The nganga said : "I'll give you a ngona horn." The nganga gave the man a ngona horn and said : "If you hunt with the ngona horn you will always bring home plenty of meat. But do not try to do too much with the ngona horn." The man went home with the ngona horn.

From then on the man enjoyed good hunting. He always brought meat home. One day he said : "There is no reason why I should always leave home. In future I shall send the ngona horn hunting alone." The man sent the ngona horn hunting. The ngona horn came back with plenty of meat. The man said to the ngona horn : "Now keep on hunting all the time and keep on bring-

Southern Rhodesian drawing.

ing home meat." The man had forgotten the words of the nganga.

The ngona horn hunted steadily and continually brought in game. Finally the house was full of meat. The man said : "I can no longer live in this house, there is so much meat in it." Some distance away the man built himself another house in the bush. But the meat in the first house made a strong smell. The smell followed the man into his new house. The man built himself a third house still further off in the bush. But the smell of the meat followed the man into his new house. The ngona horn said to the man : "When you have had enough of me, then send me back to the nganga." But the man did not send the ngona horn back to the nganga.

The man built himself a fourth house still further out in the bush. But the smell of the meat followed the man into the fourth house, too. The smell of the meat killed him.

THE FISHERMAN

Two young men said : "Let us go to another country, seek maidens and marry." The two young men set off. They came to another country. They found two maidens. They married. They built themselves houses.

One of the two young men had a horn full of oil. It was a ngona horn. One day he said to his friend : "Come with me tomorrow to the river. We will go fishing." The friend said : "Very well." The next day they went early to the river. The young man took his ngona horn with him.

When they came to the river the young man said to his friend : "I am going into the water and will come back this evening at sundown. Now when I go under the water hold the horn so that the mouth points downwards. But when the sun sets turn the horn so that the mouth points upwards." The friend said : "Good, I will do as you say." At sunrise the young man sprang into the water. His friend held the ngona horn with the mouth towards the ground. The young man stayed under water all day. When the sun set his friend turned the horn so that the mouth pointed upwards. Thereupon the young man came back out of the water. He had caught many large fish. Of these fish he gave a good share to his friend.

Early every morning the two young men went to the river. Every night they came home with plenty of fish which they gave their wives to cook. But every day the

Southern Rhodesian picture of men and canoe.

friend's wife compared her husband's fish with those of his companion. One day she asked her husband : "Why does your friend always bring home larger fish than you do ?" Her husband said : "You deceive yourself. The fish I bring home are quite enough to feed us. We have more than anyone else in the village." His wife, however, was insistent and said : "Your friend is cheating you."

One evening the young man came out of the water again and laid his catch on the sand. He divided the fish.

There was an uneven number of fish. The extra fish he kept for himself. His friend said : "My wife is right." He became very angry. But he said nothing.

However, the next day at sunset while the young man was under the water his friend did not turn the horn but kept on holding it with its mouth towards the ground. And then the young man under the water died.

THE WATER LIONS

In a village there lived nine unmarried maidens and they were friends. One day one of the nine became pregnant. The other eight maidens said : "Why is she pregnant when we are not ?" The eight maidens were jealous. The ninth maiden bore a child. The other eight maidens said : "Why has this maiden a child when we have none ?" The other eight maidens said: "Let us go bathing with her. Let us persuade her to throw the child into the water."

The eight maidens said to the ninth maiden: "Come with us, we want to go bathing." The ninth maiden went with the others, the child on her back. When they came to the water the eight maidens said to the ninth : "Throw your child into the water. The child is not good for you. For you are no older than we and we have no children. You are not old enough to have a child." The ninth maiden let herself be persuaded. The ninth maiden threw her child into the water. Lions lived under the water. They caught the child as it sank and put it in a large jar.

When the ninth maiden returned to the village her parents asked: "Where is the child ?" The maiden said : "I have thrown the child into the water." Her parents asked : "Why have you thrown the child into the water ?" The maiden answered: "The other maidens said, 'Throw your child into the water. You are no older than we and we have no children.' " The young man, the father of the child, heard that the maiden had thrown his child into the water. The young man came. The young man and the parents scolded the maiden.

The maiden ran away. She ran to the pond into which she had thrown the child. The maiden jumped into the water. The father of the child fetched his ngona horn and ran after the maiden. The young man came to the pond. The young man sprang into the pond with his ngona horn. Under the water the young man met the maiden. The young man asked the maiden : "Have you seen my child ?" The maiden said : "I have not yet seen your child." The young man and the maiden walked along under the water.

The young man and the maiden met the lions. The young man asked the lions : "Have you seen my child ? This maiden has thrown my child into the water." The lions said : "We have put the child in a jar. Can you tell which jar it is ?" The young man said : "Yes, I can tell which jar it is." One of the lions said : "Come with me." The lion led the young man and the maiden to a row of large jars. The lion said : "Now guess in which jar your child is. If you make a false guess we will not give you back the child." The young man looked at the jars. The young man asked his ngona horn. The ngona horn told him. The young man pointed to the jar in which the child was.

The lion said : "We give you back your child. Stay here. Wait till the child has grown up. Then we will eat all of you." The lions went hunting. The young man said to the maiden : "I will put you in the ngona horn. I will put the child in the ngona horn." The young man opened the top of the ngona horn. The young man pushed the maiden into the ngona horn. The young man put the child into the ngona horn. He climbed into the ngona horn himself and pulled the stopper into place behind him.

The lions came back from hunting. The lions asked : "Where are the young man, the maiden and the child ?" The lions searched. The lions were unable to find the young man, the maiden and the child. The lions said : "The young man and the maiden have run away." One of the lions found the ngona horn. The lion said : "The young man has forgotten something." The lion was angry. The lion took the ngona horn and threw it up through the water and on to the shore.

The young man, the maiden and the child came out of the ngona horn. The maiden took the ngona horn on her back. The young man and the maiden went to the village. The young man married the maiden.

Wahungwe Legend

MBILA

A long, long time ago no rain fell for a whole year. Thereupon the Wanganga ordered that a Mukaranga be sacrified. The Wanganga said : "It must be a marriageable Musarre (princess) who has never lain with a man. The Musarre must be virgin." The Mambo called his first wife and said : "Seek among the Musarre for one who is marriageable and innocent of man, one whom we can sacrifice." The king's first wife summoned all the Wasarre (princesses, plural of Musarra) and asked : "Which of you has not yet slept with a man ?" The king's daughters laughed and said : "Is it our business to live as other maidens live ?" The king's first wife said : "Lie down." The Wasarre lay down, each on a mat. The king's first wife found among the marriageable Wasarre not one who had not had intercourse with a man.

The king's first wife went to the king and said : "Mambo, among the marriageable Wasarre there is not one who has not had intercourse with a man." The king summoned the Wanganga and said : "Among the Wasarre is not one who has not had intercourse with a man. Tell me, what shall be done ?" The Wanganga said : "Mambo, the Mukaranga must be sacrificed. If there is

no marriageable Musarre who is still innocent of man,
then we must seek the oldest of the Wasarre who have not
yet reached marriageable age. This Musarre must be im-
prisoned at the place of sacrifice and must remain im-
prisoned till she has reached a marriageable age. And then
she can be sacrificed as a Mukaranga." The king called his
first wife and said : "Seek among the unmarriageable
Wasarre for a Musarre who is innocent of man." The
king's first wife summoned the small girls of the Sim-
bawoye (royal court). She found a child who was still
innocent of man. Her breasts were not yet grown.

The young Musarre was brought to the place of sacrifice. The place of sacrifice was a high wall (circular, like
that of a hut, and with an entrance. The wall was built
not of wood and mud but of stone). In the centre stood
a large antheap. On the antheap grew a tree. The maiden
was brought into the place of sacrifice. The entrance was
closed with heavy stones. Every day the grown Wasarre
brought the Mukaranga food and drink. They handed
it down over the wall. The Wakaranga kept watch to see
that no man approached the place of sacrifice.

The maiden grew. Two years passed before the maiden
was grown and had breasts. In the course of these two
years no rain fell. All the cattle died. Many people died.
The rivers dried up. The grain did not take root. One day
the maiden was marriageable.

The Wanganga went to the king. The Wanganga
said : "The Mukaranga is marriageable. The Mbila can
begin." The king summoned all his people. The people

South Rhodesian ceremonial dance picture.

gathered at the place of sacrifice. The Wanganga opened
the entrance to the place of sacrifice. The Wanganga dug
out a chamber beneath the roots of the tree on the
antheap. The Wanganga shouted (sang) the Mizimu.*
The Wanganga strangled the Mukaranga. The people
danced around the place of sacrifice. The Wanganga
buried the maiden in the antheap beneath the roots of
the great tree. The priests shouted the Mizimu. The
people danced around the place of sacrifice.

As soon as the Mukaranga was buried beneath its roots,
the tree began to grow. The tree grew and grew. It grew
the whole night through. The tree grew for three days.
For three days the people danced. As the morning drew
near again the crown of the tree reached the sky. In the
sky there appeared the morning star (Venus) for the
first time (after having set as the evening star some time
before). The crown of the tree spread out along the sky.
One could no longer see the stars and the moon. A great
wind came. The leaves of the tree turned into clouds. It
began to rain. It rained for thirty days.

Since then the Wazezuru sacrifice a maiden whenever
there is a long drought.

* Unfortunately it was impossible to obtain the exact text of
the song.

A CATALOG OF SELECTED

DOVER BOOKS

IN ALL FIELDS OF INTEREST

A CATALOG OF SELECTED DOVER
BOOKS IN ALL FIELDS OF INTEREST

CONCERNING THE SPIRITUAL IN ART, Wassily Kandinsky. Pioneering work by father of abstract art. Thoughts on color theory, nature of art. Analysis of earlier masters. 12 illustrations. 80pp. of text. 5⅜ x 8½. 23411-8 Pa. $4.95

ANIMALS: 1,419 Copyright-Free Illustrations of Mammals, Birds, Fish, Insects, etc., Jim Harter (ed.). Clear wood engravings present, in extremely lifelike poses, over 1,000 species of animals. One of the most extensive pictorial sourcebooks of its kind. Captions. Index. 284pp. 9 x 12. 23766-4 Pa. $14.95

CELTIC ART: The Methods of Construction, George Bain. Simple geometric techniques for making Celtic interlacements, spirals, Kells-type initials, animals, humans, etc. Over 500 illustrations. 160pp. 9 x 12. (USO) 22923-8 Pa. $9.95

AN ATLAS OF ANATOMY FOR ARTISTS, Fritz Schider. Most thorough reference work on art anatomy in the world. Hundreds of illustrations, including selections from works by Vesalius, Leonardo, Goya, Ingres, Michelangelo, others. 593 illustrations. 192pp. 7⅛ x 10¼. 20241-0 Pa. $9.95

CELTIC HAND STROKE-BY-STROKE (Irish Half-Uncial from "The Book of Kells"): An Arthur Baker Calligraphy Manual, Arthur Baker. Complete guide to creating each letter of the alphabet in distinctive Celtic manner. Covers hand position, strokes, pens, inks, paper, more. Illustrated. 48pp. 8¼ x 11. 24336-2 Pa. $3.95

EASY ORIGAMI, John Montroll. Charming collection of 32 projects (hat, cup, pelican, piano, swan, many more) specially designed for the novice origami hobbyist. Clearly illustrated easy-to-follow instructions insure that even beginning papercrafters will achieve successful results. 48pp. 8¼ x 11. 27298-2 Pa. $3.50

THE COMPLETE BOOK OF BIRDHOUSE CONSTRUCTION FOR WOODWORKERS, Scott D. Campbell. Detailed instructions, illustrations, tables. Also data on bird habitat and instinct patterns. Bibliography. 3 tables. 63 illustrations in 15 figures. 48pp. 5¼ x 8½. 24407-5 Pa. $2.50

BLOOMINGDALE'S ILLUSTRATED 1886 CATALOG: Fashions, Dry Goods and Housewares, Bloomingdale Brothers. Famed merchants' extremely rare catalog depicting about 1,700 products: clothing, housewares, firearms, dry goods, jewelry, more. Invaluable for dating, identifying vintage items. Also, copyright-free graphics for artists, designers. Co-published with Henry Ford Museum & Greenfield Village. 160pp. 8¼ x 11. 25780-0 Pa. $10.95

HISTORIC COSTUME IN PICTURES, Braun & Schneider. Over 1,450 costumed figures in clearly detailed engravings–from dawn of civilization to end of 19th century. Captions. Many folk costumes. 256pp. 8⅜ x 11¾. 23150-X Pa. $12.95

STICKLEY CRAFTSMAN FURNITURE CATALOGS, Gustav Stickley and L. & J. G. Stickley. Beautiful, functional furniture in two authentic catalogs from 1910. 594 illustrations, including 277 photos, show settles, rockers, armchairs, reclining chairs, bookcases, desks, tables. 183pp. 6½ x 9¼. 23838-5 Pa. $11.95

AMERICAN LOCOMOTIVES IN HISTORIC PHOTOGRAPHS: 1858 to 1949, Ron Ziel (ed.). A rare collection of 126 meticulously detailed official photographs, called "builder portraits," of American locomotives that majestically chronicle the rise of steam locomotive power in America. Introduction. Detailed captions. xi + 129pp. 9 x 12. 27393-8 Pa. $13.95

AMERICA'S LIGHTHOUSES: An Illustrated History, Francis Ross Holland, Jr. Delightfully written, profusely illustrated fact-filled survey of over 200 American lighthouses since 1716. History, anecdotes, technological advances, more. 240pp. 8 x 10¾. 25576-X Pa. $12.95

TOWARDS A NEW ARCHITECTURE, Le Corbusier. Pioneering manifesto by founder of "International School." Technical and aesthetic theories, views of industry, economics, relation of form to function, "mass-production split" and much more. Profusely illustrated. 320pp. 6⅛ x 9¼. (USO) 25023-7 Pa. $9.95

HOW THE OTHER HALF LIVES, Jacob Riis. Famous journalistic record, exposing poverty and degradation of New York slums around 1900, by major social reformer. 100 striking and influential photographs. 233pp. 10 x 7⅞. 22012-5 Pa. $11.95

FRUIT KEY AND TWIG KEY TO TREES AND SHRUBS, William M. Harlow. One of the handiest and most widely used identification aids. Fruit key covers 120 deciduous and evergreen species; twig key 160 deciduous species. Easily used. Over 300 photographs. 126pp. 5⅜ x 8½. 20511-8 Pa. $3.95

COMMON BIRD SONGS, Dr. Donald J. Borror. Songs of 60 most common U.S. birds: robins, sparrows, cardinals, bluejays, finches, more—arranged in order of increasing complexity. Up to 9 variations of songs of each species.
Cassette and manual 99911-4 $8.95

ORCHIDS AS HOUSE PLANTS, Rebecca Tyson Northen. Grow cattleyas and many other kinds of orchids—in a window, in a case, or under artificial light. 63 illustrations. 148pp. 5⅜ x 8½. 23261-1 Pa. $5.95

MONSTER MAZES, Dave Phillips. Masterful mazes at four levels of difficulty. Avoid deadly perils and evil creatures to find magical treasures. Solutions for all 32 exciting illustrated puzzles. 48pp. 8¼ x 11. 26005-4 Pa. $2.95

MOZART'S DON GIOVANNI (DOVER OPERA LIBRETTO SERIES), Wolfgang Amadeus Mozart. Introduced and translated by Ellen H. Bleiler. Standard Italian libretto, with complete English translation. Convenient and thoroughly portable—an ideal companion for reading along with a recording or the performance itself. Introduction. List of characters. Plot summary. 121pp. 5¼ x 8½. 24944-1 Pa. $3.95

TECHNICAL MANUAL AND DICTIONARY OF CLASSICAL BALLET, Gail Grant. Defines, explains, comments on steps, movements, poses and concepts. 15-page pictorial section. Basic book for student, viewer. 127pp. 5⅜ x 8½. 21843-0 Pa. $4.95

BRASS INSTRUMENTS: Their History and Development, Anthony Baines. Authoritative, updated survey of the evolution of trumpets, trombones, bugles, cornets, French horns, tubas and other brass wind instruments. Over 140 illustrations and 48 music examples. Corrected and updated by author. New preface. Bibliography. 320pp. 5$\frac{3}{8}$ x 8$\frac{1}{2}$. 27574-4 Pa. $9.95

HOLLYWOOD GLAMOR PORTRAITS, John Kobal (ed.). 145 photos from 1926-49. Harlow, Gable, Bogart, Bacall; 94 stars in all. Full background on photographers, technical aspects. 160pp. 8$\frac{3}{8}$ x 11$\frac{1}{4}$. 23352-9 Pa. $12.95

MAX AND MORITZ, Wilhelm Busch. Great humor classic in both German and English. Also 10 other works: "Cat and Mouse," "Plisch and Plumm," etc. 216pp. 5$\frac{3}{8}$ x 8$\frac{1}{2}$. 20181-3 Pa. $6.95

THE RAVEN AND OTHER FAVORITE POEMS, Edgar Allan Poe. Over 40 of the author's most memorable poems: "The Bells," "Ulalume," "Israfel," "To Helen," "The Conqueror Worm," "Eldorado," "Annabel Lee," many more. Alphabetic lists of titles and first lines. 64pp. 5$\frac{3}{16}$ x 8$\frac{1}{4}$. 26685-0 Pa. $1.00

PERSONAL MEMOIRS OF U. S. GRANT, Ulysses Simpson Grant. Intelligent, deeply moving firsthand account of Civil War campaigns, considered by many the finest military memoirs ever written. Includes letters, historic photographs, maps and more. 528pp. 6$\frac{1}{8}$ x 9$\frac{1}{4}$. 28587-1 Pa. $12.95

AMULETS AND SUPERSTITIONS, E. A. Wallis Budge. Comprehensive discourse on origin, powers of amulets in many ancient cultures: Arab, Persian Babylonian, Assyrian, Egyptian, Gnostic, Hebrew, Phoenician, Syriac, etc. Covers cross, swastika, crucifix, seals, rings, stones, etc. 584pp. 5$\frac{3}{8}$ x 8$\frac{1}{2}$. 23573-4 Pa. $15.95

RUSSIAN STORIES/PYCCKNE PACCKA3bl: A Dual-Language Book, edited by Gleb Struve. Twelve tales by such masters as Chekhov, Tolstoy, Dostoevsky, Pushkin, others. Excellent word-for-word English translations on facing pages, plus teaching and study aids, Russian/English vocabulary, biographical/critical introductions, more. 416pp. 5$\frac{3}{8}$ x 8$\frac{1}{2}$. 26244-8 Pa. $9.95

PHILADELPHIA THEN AND NOW: 60 Sites Photographed in the Past and Present, Kenneth Finkel and Susan Oyama. Rare photographs of City Hall, Logan Square, Independence Hall, Betsy Ross House, other landmarks juxtaposed with contemporary views. Captures changing face of historic city. Introduction. Captions. 128pp. 8$\frac{1}{4}$ x 11. 25790-8 Pa. $9.95

AIA ARCHITECTURAL GUIDE TO NASSAU AND SUFFOLK COUNTIES, LONG ISLAND, The American Institute of Architects, Long Island Chapter, and the Society for the Preservation of Long Island Antiquities. Comprehensive, well-researched and generously illustrated volume brings to life over three centuries of Long Island's great architectural heritage. More than 240 photographs with authoritative, extensively detailed captions. 176pp. 8$\frac{1}{4}$ x 11. 26946-9 Pa. $14.95

NORTH AMERICAN INDIAN LIFE: Customs and Traditions of 23 Tribes, Elsie Clews Parsons (ed.). 27 fictionalized essays by noted anthropologists examine religion, customs, government, additional facets of life among the Winnebago, Crow, Zuni, Eskimo, other tribes. 480pp. 6$\frac{1}{8}$ x 9$\frac{1}{4}$. 27377-6 Pa. $10.95

FRANK LLOYD WRIGHT'S HOLLYHOCK HOUSE, Donald Hoffmann. Lavishly illustrated, carefully documented study of one of Wright's most controversial residential designs. Over 120 photographs, floor plans, elevations, etc. Detailed perceptive text by noted Wright scholar. Index. 128pp. 9¼ x 10¾. 27133-1 Pa. $11.95

THE MALE AND FEMALE FIGURE IN MOTION: 60 Classic Photographic Sequences, Eadweard Muybridge. 60 true-action photographs of men and women walking, running, climbing, bending, turning, etc., reproduced from rare 19th-century masterpiece. vi + 121pp. 9 x 12. 24745-7 Pa. $10.95

1001 QUESTIONS ANSWERED ABOUT THE SEASHORE, N. J. Berrill and Jacquelyn Berrill. Queries answered about dolphins, sea snails, sponges, starfish, fishes, shore birds, many others. Covers appearance, breeding, growth, feeding, much more. 305pp. 5¼ x 8¼. 23366-9 Pa. $9.95

GUIDE TO OWL WATCHING IN NORTH AMERICA, Donald S. Heintzelman. Superb guide offers complete data and descriptions of 19 species: barn owl, screech owl, snowy owl, many more. Expert coverage of owl-watching equipment, conservation, migrations and invasions, etc. Guide to observing sites. 84 illustrations. xiii + 193pp. 5⅜ x 8½. 27344-X Pa. $8.95

MEDICINAL AND OTHER USES OF NORTH AMERICAN PLANTS: A Historical Survey with Special Reference to the Eastern Indian Tribes, Charlotte Erichsen-Brown. Chronological historical citations document 500 years of usage of plants, trees, shrubs native to eastern Canada, northeastern U.S. Also complete identifying information. 343 illustrations. 544pp. 6½ x 9¼. 25951-X Pa. $12.95

STORYBOOK MAZES, Dave Phillips. 23 stories and mazes on two-page spreads: Wizard of Oz, Treasure Island, Robin Hood, etc. Solutions. 64pp. 8¼ x 11. 23628-5 Pa. $2.95

NEGRO FOLK MUSIC, U.S.A., Harold Courlander. Noted folklorist's scholarly yet readable analysis of rich and varied musical tradition. Includes authentic versions of over 40 folk songs. Valuable bibliography and discography. xi + 324pp. 5⅜ x 8½. 27350-4 Pa. $9.95

MOVIE-STAR PORTRAITS OF THE FORTIES, John Kobal (ed.). 163 glamor, studio photos of 106 stars of the 1940s: Rita Hayworth, Ava Gardner, Marlon Brando, Clark Gable, many more. 176pp. 8⅜ x 11¼. 23546-7 Pa. $14.95

BENCHLEY LOST AND FOUND, Robert Benchley. Finest humor from early 30s, about pet peeves, child psychologists, post office and others. Mostly unavailable elsewhere. 73 illustrations by Peter Arno and others. 183pp. 5⅜ x 8½. 22410-4 Pa. $6.95

YEKL and THE IMPORTED BRIDEGROOM AND OTHER STORIES OF YIDDISH NEW YORK, Abraham Cahan. Film Hester Street based on Yekl (1896). Novel, other stories among first about Jewish immigrants on N.Y.'s East Side. 240pp. 5⅜ x 8½. 22427-9 Pa. $6.95

SELECTED POEMS, Walt Whitman. Generous sampling from *Leaves of Grass.* Twenty-four poems include "I Hear America Singing," "Song of the Open Road," "I Sing the Body Electric," "When Lilacs Last in the Dooryard Bloom'd," "O Captain! My Captain!"–all reprinted from an authoritative edition. Lists of titles and first lines. 128pp. 5³⁄₁₆ x 8¼. 26878 0 Pa. $1.00

PHOTOGRAPHIC SKETCHBOOK OF THE CIVIL WAR, Alexander Gardner. 100 photos taken on field during the Civil War. Famous shots of Manassas Harper's Ferry, Lincoln, Richmond, slave pens, etc. 244pp. 10⅝ x 8¼. 22731-6 Pa. $10.95

FIVE ACRES AND INDEPENDENCE, Maurice G. Kains. Great back-to-the-land classic explains basics of self-sufficient farming. The one book to get. 95 illustrations. 397pp. 5⅜ x 8½. 20974-1 Pa. $7.95

SONGS OF EASTERN BIRDS, Dr. Donald J. Borror. Songs and calls of 60 species most common to eastern U.S.: warblers, woodpeckers, flycatchers, thrushes, larks, many more in high-quality recording. Cassette and manual 99912-2 $9.95

A MODERN HERBAL, Margaret Grieve. Much the fullest, most exact, most useful compilation of herbal material. Gigantic alphabetical encyclopedia, from aconite to zedoary, gives botanical information, medical properties, folklore, economic uses, much else. Indispensable to serious reader. 161 illustrations. 888pp. 6½ x 9¼. 2-vol. set. (USO) Vol. I: 22798-7 Pa. $9.95
Vol. II: 22799-5 Pa. $9.95

HIDDEN TREASURE MAZE BOOK, Dave Phillips. Solve 34 challenging mazes accompanied by heroic tales of adventure. Evil dragons, people-eating plants, blood-thirsty giants, many more dangerous adversaries lurk at every twist and turn. 34 mazes, stories, solutions. 48pp. 8¼ x 11. 24566-7 Pa. $2.95

LETTERS OF W. A. MOZART, Wolfgang A. Mozart. Remarkable letters show bawdy wit, humor, imagination, musical insights, contemporary musical world; includes some letters from Leopold Mozart. 276pp. 5⅜ x 8½. 22859-2 Pa. $7.95

BASIC PRINCIPLES OF CLASSICAL BALLET, Agrippina Vaganova. Great Russian theoretician, teacher explains methods for teaching classical ballet. 118 illustrations. 175pp. 5⅜ x 8½. 22036-2 Pa. $5.95

THE JUMPING FROG, Mark Twain. Revenge edition. The original story of The Celebrated Jumping Frog of Calaveras County, a hapless French translation, and Twain's hilarious "retranslation" from the French. 12 illustrations. 66pp. 5⅜ x 8½. 22686-7 Pa. $3.95

BEST REMEMBERED POEMS, Martin Gardner (ed.). The 126 poems in this superb collection of 19th- and 20th-century British and American verse range from Shelley's "To a Skylark" to the impassioned "Renascence" of Edna St. Vincent Millay and to Edward Lear's whimsical "The Owl and the Pussycat." 224pp. 5⅜ x 8½. 27165-X Pa. $5.95

COMPLETE SONNETS, William Shakespeare. Over 150 exquisite poems deal with love, friendship, the tyranny of time, beauty's evanescence, death and other themes in language of remarkable power, precision and beauty. Glossary of archaic terms. 80pp. 5 3/16 x 8¼. 26686-9 Pa. $1.00

BODIES IN A BOOKSHOP, R. T. Campbell. Challenging mystery of blackmail and murder with ingenious plot and superbly drawn characters. In the best tradition of British suspense fiction. 192pp. 5⅜ x 8½. 24720-1 Pa. $6.95

THE WIT AND HUMOR OF OSCAR WILDE, Alvin Redman (ed.). More than 1,000 ripostes, paradoxes, wisecracks: Work is the curse of the drinking classes; I can resist everything except temptation; etc. 258pp. 5⅜ x 8½.   20602-5 Pa. $6.95

SHAKESPEARE LEXICON AND QUOTATION DICTIONARY, Alexander Schmidt. Full definitions, locations, shades of meaning in every word in plays and poems. More than 50,000 exact quotations. 1,485pp. 6½ x 9¼. 2-vol. set.
Vol. 1: 22726-X Pa. $17.95
Vol. 2: 22727-8 Pa. $17.95

SELECTED POEMS, Emily Dickinson. Over 100 best-known, best-loved poems by one of America's foremost poets, reprinted from authoritative early editions. No comparable edition at this price. Index of first lines. 64pp. 5³⁄₁₆ x 8¼.
26466-1 Pa. $1.00

CELEBRATED CASES OF JUDGE DEE (DEE GOONG AN), translated by Robert van Gulik. Authentic 18th-century Chinese detective novel; Dee and associates solve three interlocked cases. Led to van Gulik's own stories with same characters. Extensive introduction. 9 illustrations. 237pp. 5⅜ x 8½.   23337-5 Pa. $7.95

THE MALLEUS MALEFICARUM OF KRAMER AND SPRENGER, translated by Montague Summers. Full text of most important witchhunter's "bible," used by both Catholics and Protestants. 278pp. 6⅝ x 10.   22802-9 Pa. $12.95

SPANISH STORIES/CUENTOS ESPAÑOLES: A Dual-Language Book, Angel Flores (ed.). Unique format offers 13 great stories in Spanish by Cervantes, Borges, others. Faithful English translations on facing pages. 352pp. 5⅜ x 8½.
25399-6 Pa. $8.95

THE CHICAGO WORLD'S FAIR OF 1893: A Photographic Record, Stanley Appelbaum (ed.). 128 rare photos show 200 buildings, Beaux-Arts architecture, Midway, original Ferris Wheel, Edison's kinetoscope, more. Architectural emphasis; full text. 116pp. 8¼ x 11.   23990-X Pa. $9.95

OLD QUEENS, N.Y., IN EARLY PHOTOGRAPHS, Vincent F. Seyfried and William Asadorian. Over 160 rare photographs of Maspeth, Jamaica, Jackson Heights, and other areas. Vintage views of DeWitt Clinton mansion, 1939 World's Fair and more. Captions. 192pp. 8⅞ x 11.   26358-4 Pa. $12.95

CAPTURED BY THE INDIANS: 15 Firsthand Accounts, 1750-1870, Frederick Drimmer. Astounding true historical accounts of grisly torture, bloody conflicts, relentless pursuits, miraculous escapes and more, by people who lived to tell the tale. 384pp. 5⅜ x 8½.   24901-8 Pa. $8.95

THE WORLD'S GREAT SPEECHES, Lewis Copeland and Lawrence W. Lamm (eds.). Vast collection of 278 speeches of Greeks to 1970. Powerful and effective models; unique look at history. 842pp. 5⅜ x 8½.   20468-5 Pa. $14.95

THE BOOK OF THE SWORD, Sir Richard F. Burton. Great Victorian scholar/adventurer's eloquent, erudite history of the "queen of weapons"—from prehistory to early Roman Empire. Evolution and development of early swords, variations (sabre, broadsword, cutlass, scimitar, etc.), much more. 336pp. 6⅛ x 9¼.
25434-8 Pa. $9.95

AUTOBIOGRAPHY: The Story of My Experiments with Truth, Mohandas K. Gandhi. Boyhood, legal studies, purification, the growth of the Satyagraha (nonviolent protest) movement. Critical, inspiring work of the man responsible for the freedom of India. 480pp. 5⅜ x 8½. (USO) 24593-4 Pa. $8.95

CELTIC MYTHS AND LEGENDS, T. W. Rolleston. Masterful retelling of Irish and Welsh stories and tales. Cuchulain, King Arthur, Deirdre, the Grail, many more. First paperback edition. 58 full-page illustrations. 512pp. 5⅜ x 8½. 26507-2 Pa. $9.95

THE PRINCIPLES OF PSYCHOLOGY, William James. Famous long course complete, unabridged. Stream of thought, time perception, memory, experimental methods; great work decades ahead of its time. 94 figures. 1,391pp. 5⅜ x 8½. 2-vol. set.
Vol. I: 20381-6 Pa. $13.95
Vol. II: 20382-4 Pa. $14.95

THE WORLD AS WILL AND REPRESENTATION, Arthur Schopenhauer. Definitive English translation of Schopenhauer's life work, correcting more than 1,000 errors, omissions in earlier translations. Translated by E. F. J. Payne. Total of 1,269pp. 5⅜ x 8½. 2-vol. set.
Vol. 1: 21761-2 Pa. $12.95
Vol. 2: 21762-0 Pa. $12.95

MAGIC AND MYSTERY IN TIBET, Madame Alexandra David-Neel. Experiences among lamas, magicians, sages, sorcerers, Bonpa wizards. A true psychic discovery. 32 illustrations. 321pp. 5⅜ x 8½. (USO) 22682-4 Pa. $9.95

THE EGYPTIAN BOOK OF THE DEAD, E. A. Wallis Budge. Complete reproduction of Ani's papyrus, finest ever found. Full hieroglyphic text, interlinear transliteration, word-for-word translation, smooth translation. 533pp. 6½ x 9¼.
21866-X Pa. $11.95

MATHEMATICS FOR THE NONMATHEMATICIAN, Morris Kline. Detailed, college-level treatment of mathematics in cultural and historical context, with numerous exercises. Recommended Reading Lists. Tables. Numerous figures. 641pp. 5⅜ x 8½.
24823-2 Pa. $11.95

THEORY OF WING SECTIONS: Including a Summary of Airfoil Data, Ira H. Abbott and A. E. von Doenhoff. Concise compilation of subsonic aerodynamic characteristics of NACA wing sections, plus description of theory. 350pp. of tables. 693pp. 5⅜ x 8½. 60586-8 Pa. $14.95

THE RIME OF THE ANCIENT MARINER, Gustave Doré, S. T. Coleridge. Doré's finest work; 34 plates capture moods, subtleties of poem. Flawless full-size reproductions printed on facing pages with authoritative text of poem. "Beautiful. Simply beautiful."–*Publisher's Weekly*. 77pp. 9¼ x 12. 22305-1 Pa. $7.95

NORTH AMERICAN INDIAN DESIGNS FOR ARTISTS AND CRAFTSPEOPLE, Eva Wilson. Over 360 authentic copyright-free designs adapted from Navajo blankets, Hopi pottery, Sioux buffalo hides, more. Geometrics, symbolic figures, plant and animal motifs, etc. 128pp. 8⅜ x 11. (EUK) 25341-4 Pa. $8.95

SCULPTURE: Principles and Practice, Louis Slobodkin. Step-by-step approach to clay, plaster, metals, stone; classical and modern. 253 drawings, photos. 255pp. 8⅛ x 11.
22960-2 Pa. $11.95

THE INFLUENCE OF SEA POWER UPON HISTORY, 1660–1783, A. T. Mahan. Influential classic of naval history and tactics still used as text in war colleges. First paperback edition. 4 maps. 24 battle plans. 640pp. 5⅜ x 8½. 25509-3 Pa. $14.95

THE STORY OF THE TITANIC AS TOLD BY ITS SURVIVORS, Jack Winocour (ed.). What it was really like. Panic, despair, shocking inefficiency, and a little heroism. More thrilling than any fictional account. 26 illustrations. 320pp. 5⅜ x 8½. 20610-6 Pa. $8.95

FAIRY AND FOLK TALES OF THE IRISH PEASANTRY, William Butler Yeats (ed.). Treasury of 64 tales from the twilight world of Celtic myth and legend: "The Soul Cages," "The Kildare Pooka," "King O'Toole and his Goose," many more. Introduction and Notes by W. B. Yeats. 352pp. 5⅜ x 8½. 26941-8 Pa. $8.95

BUDDHIST MAHAYANA TEXTS, E. B. Cowell and Others (eds.). Superb, accurate translations of basic documents in Mahayana Buddhism, highly important in history of religions. The Buddha-karita of Asvaghosha, Larger Sukhavativyuha, more. 448pp. 5⅜ x 8½. 25552-2 Pa. $12.95

ONE TWO THREE . . . INFINITY: Facts and Speculations of Science, George Gamow. Great physicist's fascinating, readable overview of contemporary science: number theory, relativity, fourth dimension, entropy, genes, atomic structure, much more. 128 illustrations. Index. 352pp. 5⅜ x 8½. 25664-2 Pa. $8.95

ENGINEERING IN HISTORY, Richard Shelton Kirby, et al. Broad, nontechnical survey of history's major technological advances: birth of Greek science, industrial revolution, electricity and applied science, 20th-century automation, much more. 181 illustrations. ". . . excellent . . ."–*Isis.* Bibliography. vii + 530pp. 5⅜ x 8¼. 26412-2 Pa. $14.95

DALÍ ON MODERN ART: The Cuckolds of Antiquated Modern Art, Salvador Dalí. Influential painter skewers modern art and its practitioners. Outrageous evaluations of Picasso, Cézanne, Turner, more. 15 renderings of paintings discussed. 44 calligraphic decorations by Dalí. 96pp. 5⅜ x 8½. (USO) 29220-7 Pa. $4.95

ANTIQUE PLAYING CARDS: A Pictorial History, Henry René D'Allemagne. Over 900 elaborate, decorative images from rare playing cards (14th–20th centuries): Bacchus, death, dancing dogs, hunting scenes, royal coats of arms, players cheating, much more. 96pp. 9¼ x 12¼. 29265-7 Pa. $12.95

MAKING FURNITURE MASTERPIECES: 30 Projects with Measured Drawings, Franklin H. Gottshall. Step-by-step instructions, illustrations for constructing handsome, useful pieces, among them a Sheraton desk, Chippendale chair, Spanish desk, Queen Anne table and a William and Mary dressing mirror. 224pp. 8⅛ x 11¼. 29338-6 Pa. $13.95

THE FOSSIL BOOK: A Record of Prehistoric Life, Patricia V. Rich et al. Profusely illustrated definitive guide covers everything from single-celled organisms and dinosaurs to birds and mammals and the interplay between climate and man. Over 1,500 illustrations. 760pp. 7½ x 10⅛. 29371-8 Pa. $29.95

Prices subject to change without notice.

Available at your book dealer or write for free catalog to Dept. GI, Dover Publications, Inc., 31 East 2nd St., Mineola, N.Y. 11501. Dover publishes more than 500 books each year on science, elementary and advanced mathematics, biology, music, art, literary history, social sciences and other areas.